WAKING

SLEEPING

BEAUTY

WAKING

SLEEPING

BEAUTY

FEMINIST VOICES IN

CHILDREN'S NOVELS

BY

ROBERTA

SEELINGER

TRITES

UNIVERSITY OF IOWA PRESS

IOWA CITY

University of Iowa Press, Iowa City 52242
Copyright © 1997 by the University of Iowa Press
All rights reserved
Printed in the United States of America

http://www.uiowa.edu/~uipress

Printed on acid-free paper

Library of Congress Cataloging-in-Publication Data
Trites, Roberta Seelinger
    Waking Sleeping Beauty: feminist voices in children's
novels / by Roberta Seelinger Trites.
        p.   cm.
    Includes bibliographical references (p.   ) and index.
    ISBN 0-87745-590-2, ISBN 0-87745-591-0 (pbk.)
    1. Children's stories—History and criticism.   2. Feminism
and literature.   3. Women and literature.   4. Sex role in
literature.   I. Title.
    PN3426.C5T75   1997
    809'.89282'082—dc21   96-54875

02 01 00 99 98 97 C 5 4 3 2 1
02 01 00 99 98 97 P 5 4 3 2 1

For my children,

in the hope that they

will grow up to be

feminists, too

CONTENTS

PREFACE

No organized social movement has affected children's literature as significantly as feminism has. Since the resurgence of the women's movement in the 1960s, many children's novels published in the English language have reflected the goals of the movement. Girl protagonists, for example, have often been more active and vocal than their counterparts in earlier literature. They have had more options for adventures outside the home, for forming more varied friendships, and for setting diverse goals. As a result, their narratives have had more complexity. The majority of novels about girls no longer focus so pointedly on socializing girls into traditional femininity as books like *Charlotte's Web* (1952) did. Perhaps if White had written *Charlotte's Web* with his consciousness raised by feminism, Fern might not have had to sacrifice her childhood friends in the barn for the sake of pursuing a relationship with Henry Fussy.

Indeed, the resourcefulness that I suggest Fern needed to develop so that she could maintain both sets of friends is one of the richest legacies of feminism.[1] Although girls like Jo in *Little Women* (1868), Nancy Drew, and Anne of Green Gables have been resourceful in many children's books, only since feminism has effected a permanent change in the way our culture defines femininity has the resourcefulness of female characters been used by the character to bolster her own self-image. Jo and Nancy and Anne think much more about solving other people's problems and making other people happy than they do about garnering their strength to increase their own sense of self. Protagonists in novels influenced by feminism, however, have slowly evolved an ability to think about their place in the community without becoming so community-oriented that they become self-effacing. The feminist protagonist cares about other people, but she cares about herself, too.

My goal in this book is to explore how feminism and childhood intersect in children's novels. This book is intended as an introduction for novices to the field of children's literature, to the theories of feminism, or to both as a demonstration of how feminism as a social movement informs children's novels and how feminism as a literary theory can help us understand those texts. I have geared the study specifically to those who work with or will work with children as teachers because it seems imperative to me that educators understand the nuances of feminism at work in literature if they are to adapt successfully feminist practices in their classrooms.

The interpretations that I make rely on numerous advances that feminist literary theory has made in the last decade. I tend to avoid some of the concerns of first-wave feminism in that I do not always point out the standard acts of sexism at work in children's books, as I feel that work has already been performed admirably by a number of feminists.[2] Instead, I rely most on those theories that emphasize the positive values of gender by focusing on the strengths that inform people's gender roles. These theories have much currency for people interested in the intersection between children and books, and in fact, some of the most cogent pieces of recent feminist criticism are critiques of children's literature.[3] But much literary theory that has not necessarily investigated children's texts can also be applied to children's novels. One of my goals in this work, then, is to make accessible to people interested in children's books some of the intersections between feminist literary theory and children's novels. I hope this book will ultimately make it possible for educators to be aware of the limitless possibilities that feminist children's novels communicate so that they can in turn communicate those possibilities to children.

As an introduction, the chapters in this book are organized by topic rather than by chronology, although within the various chapters I sometimes discuss books in the historical order in which they were published. The first chapters cover the most basic concepts of feminist criticism at work in children's literature: stereotypical gender roles and subjectivity. These concepts then provide building blocks for the more intricate theories of voice, community, and narrative structure under investigation in later chapters. Each chapter opens with a summary of the theories that are relevant to the topic under discussion; then I move to interpretations of individual novels. If the movement back and forth between theory and analysis makes this book seem at times double-voiced, it is because as I write

I am trying to balance my role as a scholar with my role as a teacher so that my knowledge of literary criticism will have practical useful-ness to other teachers of children's literature.

To investigate the effects that various dimensions of feminism have had on children's literature, I start by examining feminist forms of re/vision. I begin with an analysis in chapter 2 of how characters in children's and adolescent literature reject traditional gender roles to find self-awareness and self-acceptance in enacting more balanced values in their lives than society's prescribed gender roles might have allowed them. In chapter 3, I look at specific metaphors and uses of intertextuality that feminist authors use to depict the pro-tagonist's developing sense of subjectivity. These chapters lay the groundwork for the discussion of voice that occurs in the next four chapters. Chapter 4 investigates ways that girls learn to employ their voices to overcome cultural repression. Chapter 5 looks specifically at writing as a form of verbal empowerment for child characters. Chapters 6 and 7 explore how interrelationships between female characters serve to strengthen the female protagonist's subject posi-tion by providing her with relationships in which her voice is heard. Chapter 8 combines the study of subjectivity and voice to assess how feminists use devices of narrative structure like metafiction to express concepts of community and identity as political issues. I conclude with a discussion of how feminist critical strategies are pertinent to classrooms in which children's books are used. I hope to engage my reader's thinking about the variety of faces feminism can wear. And in the process, I hope to communicate what a positive force femi-nism is for all children.

I do not, however, wish in these chapters to establish some sort of feminist canon of children's and adolescent novels. To do so would be antithetical to my purposes. As Annette Kolodny observes in "Dancing through the Minefield":

> If literary inquiry has historically escaped chaos by establishing
> canons, then it has only substituted one mode of arbitrary action
> for another—and, in this case, at the expense of half the population.
> And if feminists openly acknowledge ourselves as pluralists, then we
> do not give up the search for patterns of opposition and connection—

probably the basis of thinking itself; what we give up is simply the arrogance of claiming that our work is either exhaustive or definitive. (19–20)

I have no desire to set up some sort of exhaustive paradigm for what a feminist children's novel should include; rather, I wish to engage in the ongoing discussion about some of the possible features of such texts. I do not wish to establish boundaries; instead, I wish to knock down the walls and open the doors and windows that make it possible for us to think about feminism's effect on children's literature in a variety of ways.

The ideas in this text have been influenced by a number of scholars and friends. I would especially like to thank Kathleen Chamberlain, Gillian Adams, Lissa Paul, Jill May, and Peter Hunt for their close readings while this work was in the manuscript stage. Elizabeth Keyser, Joel Chaston, Phyllis Bixler, Mary-Agnes Taylor, Marilynn Olson, Beverly Lyon Clark, Ian Wojcik-Andrews, Margaret Higonnet, and Mitzi Myers all read and critiqued individual chapters during various stages of development. Nancy Huse has been a constant source of support. I am grateful to all of them for their guidance.

Many of my friends and colleagues at Illinois State University have also provided intellectual and emotional support. I am lucky to have worked with a number of knowledgeable children's literature faculty at ISU, including Robin Carr, Phyllis Feaster, Jan Susina, Anita Tarr, Katharine Wright, and the late and greatly mourned Taimi Ranta. Lee Brasseur, Torri Thompson, Susan Burt (now of the University of Wisconsin–Oshkosh), Sally Parry, Bob McLaughlin, Joel Haefner, Cynthia Huff, Ron Fortune, Pam Riney-Kehrberg, Rodger Tarr, and Kay Moss have all contributed in one way or another to this text. Many undergraduate and graduate students at ISU have also articulated ideas that have influenced me. I am especially grateful to the members of the Construction of Gender in Children's Literature seminar that I taught in the fall of 1994 for helping me to define the conventions of the feminist children's *Künstlerroman*: Denise Anton Wright (who also provided invaluable library assistance), Shelly Arnold, Linda Benson, Mike Cadden, and La Vina Armstrong Twohill all played a significant role in helping me to develop the ideas that appear in chapter 5. Michelle Martin, Sue Henshon, Candy Jendro, and Vanessa Wayne were not in that seminar, but their ideas have influenced me in a number of ways. The librarians in the Teaching Materials Center of ISU's Milner Library, including Cheryl Elzy, Annette Watkins Heim, and Rosalyn Wylie, have provided me with a wide variety of feminist children's titles. And the administrative support staff of the English Department, Carol Eagan, Irene Taylor, Terri Mack, and Dona Meador, have helped me with incredible fortitude. Much of the research and writing for this project was conducted with the support of three university research grants awarded to me by ISU. Thus, I am deeply indebted to the ISU community.

Finally, this text could never have been written without the constant support and solid advice of my husband, George F. Seelinger. I owe my greatest debt of gratitude to him for his love and patience.

1. DEFINING THE FEMINIST

CHILDREN'S NOVEL

My love of feminist children's books began in the late 1960s, when I was a child who complained because Bert and Freddie Bobbsey got to have more adventures than Nan and Flossie did. While I was rereading the first book in *The Bobbsey Twins* (1904) series recently, I discovered where my sense of inequity had come from: Bert's voice is "very much the same" as Nan's, "only stronger" (10), and her four-year-old brother tells her: "Girls can't be soldiers. . . . They have to get married or be dressmakers or sten'graphers or something like that" (18). Since I was planning on getting married (to one of the Monkees, if possible) and having a career (as an emergency room doctor), I didn't much like Freddie's denying married women a career. For that matter, I can't imagine that I was too impressed with the career choices he offered, either. But I wasn't a sophisticated enough reader to understand that Freddie was contextually bound by the sexist age in which he was created; I couldn't begin to fathom that his voice was one of the agents of socialization designed to teach girls like me our place in a male-dominated society.

So I did what any rational child feminist would do. I quit reading the books that angered me and turned to those I enjoyed. Patricia Beatty was my favorite author for years because in so many of her

1

books, such as *Bonanza Girl* (1962), *The Nickel-Plated Beauty* (1964), *Me, California Perkins* (1968), and *Hail Columbia* (1970), girls were active and vocal. As an adult feminist, I find these books less satisfying. Too often, brothers silence their sisters as the Bobbsey boys do; too often, the child's quest is to help a single woman get married or a married one improve the appliances in her kitchen. But at the time, I perceived Beatty's protagonists as the fictional opposites of Nan Bobbsey because they, at least, had strong voices. The study that follows reflects my lifetime quest to find and define feminist voices in children's books.

My definition of feminism relies on a belief in the worth of all individuals. I define feminism as the premise that all people should be treated equally, regardless of gender, race, class, or religion. Thus, when girls choose to wear pink and play with dolls because they hope to grow up to be homemakers, they deserve to be treated as well as when they play chief executive officer in their spare time. The important thing is that girls—and boys—have choices and that they know they have choices. A major goal of feminism is to support women's choices, but another that is equally important is to foster societal respect for those choices. And since childhood is the time in our lives when our options seem most unlimited, it is a time when respect for choices about self and about others can have serious import. Because feminism and childhood are both imbued with issues of freedom and choice, they complement each other well. Consequently, it seems only natural that so many writers for children have adopted a set of values that allows their characters to have freedoms that writers in previous generations were unable to grant their characters.

Elaine Showalter calls the "female" novel the pinnacle of feminist writing. Showalter defines the female novelist as one whose work focuses on "*self-discovery*, a turning inward freed from some of the dependency of opposition, a search for identity" (*A Literature* 13). In a manner similar to those that Showalter identifies as "female" novels, feminist children's novels demonstrate characters "turning inward" in "a search for identity" because some form of environmental pressure has made them aware that they are not upholding socially sanctioned gender roles (*A Literature* 13). That pressure may come from family, peers, social institutions, or self-doubt, but the greatest distinguishing mark of the feminist children's novel is that the character who uses introspection to overcome her oppression almost always overcomes at least part of what is oppressing her. Feminist children's novels, on the whole then, constitute a triumphal literature.

Manifestations of feminism and its influence on children's books are not always immediately self-evident, however. The distinction of what exactly is feminist in children's literature has been obscured by the clear gender distinctions that have dominated the field since its earliest history. John Newbery's *A Little Pretty Pocket-Book* (1744), which is often labeled the first commercial children's book printed in English, was marketed with a ball for boys and a pincushion for girls, as if somehow children of different sexes would read the book differently (Townsend 19). Throughout their publishing history, children's novels have tended to be gender-linked more often than not: Maria Edgeworth, Hannah More, and Louisa May Alcott wrote "girl" books of domestic drama, while Horatio Alger, Samuel Clemens, and Robert Louis Stevenson wrote "boy" books of adventures outside the home. And those authors who were marketed for both sexes, such as E. Nesbit or Enid Blyton or Arthur Ransome, wrote adventure tales that included both male and female characters, but the males were generally more active. John Rowe Townsend demonstrates the standard practice of replicating these gender labels in children's literary criticism when he writes: "Applied to the Victorian period, the phrase 'boys' literature' brings most readily to mind the adventure stories of Ballantyne, Kingston, Stevenson and Henty. 'Girls' literature' suggests the domestic stories of Miss Charlotte M. Yonge, Mrs. Ewing, Mrs. Molesworth and others" (67). Even Townsend's different treatment in giving the women titles but omitting them from the men's names reflects the basic sexism inherent in critically trying to distinguish "girls'" from "boys'" books.

However, while these categorizations of what constitutes a "boys'" and what a "girls'" book are fairly superficial for some readers, since the most motivated readers of both genders have usually been willing to read whatever they could get their hands on, the distinction between "girls'" and "boys'" books has been and still is a very real one for publishers. If nineteenth-century girls had Alcott and the *Katy* series clearly marketed for them, twentieth-century girls have had Nancy Drew and the American Girls' series marketed just as specifically for them. Much of the reason for this separation of genders in children's literature is a result of the genre's usefulness as an ideological tool.[1] At least as early as the eighteenth century, parents and educators recognized books as a way to indoctrinate their children into socially sanctioned behaviors, and authors have met that recognition for centuries. As a result, the politics of the marketplace have determined the politics of gender in children's literature for over two hundred years. But the process of gender indoctrination has been complicated by the Jo Marches and Anne of Green Gables who share with their literary descendants characteristics of strength, articulateness, creativity, and certain amounts of social power. Thus, it is impossible to identify a specific point of time at which traits I label "feminist" began to appear in children's books. Those traits have coexisted with sexist ideologies since the genre's inception.

But since the concurrent explosion of the children's book industry and the renaissance of feminism in the 1960s, many texts for children have been published that make a point of rejecting stereotypical gender roles. In fact, one of the most notable features of contemporary children's novels is the influence that various aspects of feminism have had on them. Some feminist children's novels have overt ideological agendas: Rosa Guy's *Edith Jackson* (1978) is emphatically pro-choice; Cynthia Voigt's *When She Hollers* (1994) teaches girls to overcome sexual victimization; Carol Matas's *The Burning Time* (1994) is a feminist historical revision of witch hunting in seventeenth-century France that vilifies the men who orchestrated the mass hysteria of the witch hunts. But feminist novelists are oftentimes more subtle in how they communicate about feminism. If for Anne of Green Gables growing up means learning to silence herself, for Cassie Binegar it means finding her voice. If for Heidi true happiness lies in self-abnegation, for Dicey Tillerman it lies in self-recognition.

What is a feminist children's novel? Defined simply, it is a novel in which the main character is empowered regardless of gender. A key concept here is "regardless": in a feminist children's novel, the child's sex does not provide a permanent obstacle to her development. Although s/he will likely experience some gender-related conflicts, s/he ultimately triumphs over them. Thus, Harriet the Spy's parents may want her to learn to act more ladylike, but she still proudly embraces her identity as a writer—and she never does attend the dance school that for her parents represents institutionalized femininity.

The majority of protagonists in feminist children's novels do tend to be female because the genre is so revisionary in nature. Responding to the traditional repression of feminine power, these novels serve as a corrective, sometimes consciously and sometimes less obviously so, to the images of feminine docility that proliferated in children's novels prior to the contemporary women's movement.[2] But while the main characters of feminist children's novels tend to be female, it is also possible for them to be male. Some of the most poignant feminist children's narratives are those which recognize that traditional gender roles have been as limiting for boys as they have for girls: MacLachlan's *Arthur, for the First Time* (1980), Cleary's *Dear Mr. Henshaw* (1983), and Avi's *Nothing but the Truth* (1991) are just a few of the novels that address these issues.

A number of issues more subtle than overcoming traditional gender roles inform feminist children's novels, however. Indeed, as Lissa Paul notes, novels that engage in simple role reversal are no more feminist than their counterparts; such characters are simply "hero[es] in drag" ("Enigma Variations" 199). Anna Altmann calls such inversions "irritating and retrograde" ("Parody" 22). For instance, Maisie in Jerry Spinelli's *There's a Girl in My Hammerlock* (1991) joins the wrestling team in hopes of getting a boyfriend. She tries to transform herself into a boy, which of course does not work, and discovers that the boy she thought she liked is a jerk anyway. But trying to gain power by acting male makes her little more than a hero in drag, which is indeed irritating and retrograde. Instead of engaging in such simplistic stereotype switching, feminist characters use a variety of means, notably employing their imaginations and trickery, to enact a transcendence of gender roles (Paul, "Enigma Variations" 187–92).

Another method feminist characters use to transcend gender roles is to embrace and celebrate certain characteristics traditionally linked to femininity. Instead of completely rejecting femininity (as Maisie temporarily does in *There's a Girl in My Hammerlock*), feminist protagonists recognize and rely on traits that gave their literary foremothers strength: compassion, interconnectedness, and communication. As a matter of fact, if a rejection of all traditional gender roles were a prerequisite of a children's novel being feminist, there would be precious few books in the genre, for most feminist children's novels contain a wide variety of characters, usually adults, who perpetuate stereotypical gender roles. What I call "feminist children's novels" could then be easily criticized and dismissed for being inconsistent.

I admit that almost every novel I analyze in this text contains at least one woman trapped in a stereotypical gender role. Since these novels give voice to revisionary feminist ideologies, such presences could, on the one hand, be considered conflicting ideologies. On the other hand, the presence of traditionally depicted females could be used to serve as part of the revision, for it is only against the passive female, the silent female, the objectified female, that the feminist protagonist's achievements can be fully understood. For instance, Harriet the Spy's nanny, Ole Golly, is traditional in her decision to follow the man she loves and give up her career; the peripheral women in McKinley's *The Hero and the Crown* (1985) serve largely as housekeepers; every character in MacLachlan's *Cassie Binegar* (1982) and *Unclaimed Treasures* (1984) has a first name except for the protagonists' mothers, who are also responsible for the housekeeping. These novels are nevertheless feminist because the main character, a child, is not yet trapped in a gender role. She may be surrounded by stereotypical women, and she may even adopt some stereotypical practices herself, but she is herself never imprisoned by them; she succeeds despite them and sometimes even because of them.

The most powerful way that feminist children's novels reverse traditional gender roles, however, is by their reliance on the protagonist's agency. In these novels, the protagonist is more aware of her own agency, more aware of her ability to assert her own personality and to enact her own decisions, at the end of the novel than she has been at the beginning. Unlike her literary antecedents in such novels as *Little Women* or *Anne of Green Gables* (1908), the feminist protagonist need not squelch her individuality in order to fit into society. Instead, her agency, her individuality, her choice, and her nonconformity are affirmed and even celebrated.

Closely related to the feminist protagonist's agency is the issue of her voice, for voice often serves as a metaphor for female agency. Prefeminist novels have a deplorable number of female characters who lose their articulateness as they learn to conform to societal expectations and so lose their agency. Laura Ingalls, for example, grows out of being the forthright child she is in *The Little House in the Big Woods* (1932); by the end of *These Happy Golden Years* (1943) she holds her tongue more often than not (Mowder 15–19). Her self-silencing is clearly meant to be a mark of her maturity. Anne of Green Gables, Jo March, and Katy in *What Katy Did* (1872) all grow up and into the ladylike art of silence. Feminist protagonists, however, retain their voices. They are often more articulate by the end of the novel than they were at its inception. Whether she is writing, speaking, or communicating with other people, the protagonist of the feminist children's novel almost always understands the primacy of voice.

The feminist character's recognition of her agency and her voice invariably leads to some sort of transcendence, usually taking the form of a triumph over whatever system or stricture was repressing her. The character defeats some force of evil (sometimes magical, sometimes not), or she succeeds at a typically male task, or she comes to believe in herself despite the doubts of those around her. In that sense, these books all have the sort of subversive streak that Alison Lurie identifies as being so common in children's literature (3–15). Hélène Cixous identifies all feminine writing as subversive: "A feminine text cannot fail to be more than subversive. It is volcanic; as it is written it brings about an upheaval of the old property crust, carrier of masculine investments; there's no other way. . . . it's in order to smash everything, to shatter the framework of institutions, to blow up the law, to break up the 'truth' with laughter" ("Laugh of the Medusa" 888). Any time a character in children's literature triumphs over the social institutions that have tried to hold her down, she helps to destroy the traditions that have so long forced females to occupy the position of Other.

Cixous's metaphor of the laughing Medusa symbolizes the triumph of a woman (or a girl) who can laugh at and thus subvert the existing order. Laughter emblemizes the girl's transcendence, and her transcendence is the key to her feminism and is the greatest factor that separates her from prefeminist protagonists. She does not simply grow, she grows in power. No longer the passive "good girl" who grows into a prescribed and circumscribed social role, the feminist protagonist learns to recognize and appreciate the power of her

own voice. Her awakening is not bestowed on her by a male awak-
ener; instead, she wakes herself and discovers herself to be a strong,
independent, and articulate person. Thus, while in prefeminist novels the protagonist tends to become Sleeping Beauty in a movement
from active to passive, from vocal to silent, the feminist protagonist
remains active and celebrates her agency and her voice. This, then, is
feminism's greatest impact on children's literature: it has enabled the
awakening of the female protagonist to the positive power she holds.

A word before I go on, however, about my use of the word "power."
Feminist power is more about being aware of one's agency than it is
about controlling other people. Marilyn French describes feminist
power as having "power to" do what one wants rather than having
"power over" other people (504–12). When I describe feminist protagonists as empowered, I mean that within the text they are able to
do what they want to do, what they need to do. I most emphatically
do not mean that by having power, the feminist protagonist enacts
the age-old paradigms of power that have shaped too many societies.
I use the term "power," then, to refer to positive forms of autonomy,
self-expression, and self-awareness.

My study focuses on those novels that best support the theories I
am trying to elucidate. To make my points, I provide close readings
of the novels that demonstrate these theories at work. (When I quote
from the novels, I note when I have added italics for emphasis; any
other use of italics reflects the typesetting of the original text.) My
theories have evolved from a dialogic process of reading novels and
literary criticism, noting novels' feminist characteristics, discussing
my opinions with students and colleagues and listening to theirs,
looking for more novels that display these characteristics, and then
discovering still more feminist characteristics. As a result, the novels
I have analyzed seem to me to exist in a dialogue; if they do not directly comment on each other, they certainly do seem to influence
each other. And certain novelists seem to me to have had the strongest
voices in this conversation. Virginia Hamilton, Patricia MacLachlan,
and Cynthia Voigt are among the leaders in the genre; they are
women who often write about girls who enact their agency in a multitude of ways. Thus, I analyze a number of novels by these authors.
Because of space limitations, I have only been able to include a few
novels by other major feminists such as Francesca Lia Block, Ursula K.

Le Guin, Janet Lunn, Margaret Mahy, Mildred Taylor, and Barbara Wersba. But since my text is meant to be in no way canon forming, my omission of a novel does not mark it as somehow unresponsive to feminist concerns. I hope, in fact, that this work will pave the way for many more novels to be identified and used, especially in the classroom, as feminist texts.

Many of the texts I use to make my argument are written by women of color. This is no accident, for some of the strongest feminist voices come from those who have been doubly oppressed by gender and by race. Rosa Guy, Virginia Hamilton, Angela Johnson, Minfong Ho, Nicholasa Mohr, and Mildred Taylor are only a few of the writers whose voices have communicated the urgency of including the experiences of all females in children's literature. Such critics as Rudine Sims Bishop, Violet Harris, bell hooks, Dianne Johnson-Feelings, Trinh T. Minh-Ha, Donnarae MacCann, Opal Moore, Sonia Nieto, Barbara Smith, Gayatri Chakravorty Spivak, Alice Walker, Gloria Woodard, and Yvonne Yarbro-Bejarano have taught me that any analysis that does not include multicultural voices is incomplete and inadequate. Feminism should have as much to say to children of color as it does to the white children on whom children's literary criticism all too often focuses.

Ultimately, the effect of feminism on children's literature is to create a corpus of literature that can speak to readers of all races and both genders. Peter Hunt notes that in children's literature, "questions of control, and other techniques through which power is exercised over, or shared with the reader," are of utmost importance (81). Feminist children's texts, perhaps more than any other type of children's literature, are fundamentally concerned with exactly these issues of control. In providing innumerable images of transcendent females and a multitude of ways for those transcendences to be interpreted, feminist children's novels constitute a genre concerned at the most basic level with making the reader aware of how and when she is controlled. Above all else, feminist children's novels use techniques both simple and sophisticated to call the reader to awaken herself and to reject the role of Sleeping Beauty.

2.   SUBVERTING STEREOTYPES:

REJECTING TRADITIONAL

GENDER ROLES

In the nineteenth and much of the twentieth centuries, girls in children's books seemed to have more freedom than the real girls who were their actual counterparts in British and North American cultures. For instance, in *Early Lessons* (1801) by Maria Edgeworth, Roseamonde often acts upon her own instincts, even though they get her in trouble. Later in the century, Jo March revels in her rebelliousness in *Little Women*. Mary Lennox gains much power over the denizens of Misselthwaite Manor in *The Secret Garden* (1911), and Nancy Drew has served as a role model for girls throughout this century for appearing to take charge of any situation she encounters. One set of critics, Mary Cadogan and Patricia Craig, even imply that Nancy's resourcefulness makes her almost transsexual when they maintain that "for all practical purposes" Nancy Drew *is* male because, among her other talents, she can drive cars, boats, and airplanes and "stun a would-be kidnapper with a single blow" (150). Historically, however, one of the strongest subcurrents of children's literature has been the reformation of these female rebels. Roseamonde eventually learns to be as rational as her mother wants her to be (Myers, "Dilemmas of Gender" 71–75); Jo effectively silences herself (Estes and Lant 120); Mary is supplanted in her garden by Colin (Paul, "Enigma Variations" 195); and Nancy Drew is little more than a pawn of the patriarchy (Parry 3).

Feminism's most obvious contribution to children's literature lies in the ways that female protagonists have been liberated from inevitably growing into passivity. No longer subjected to societal subjugation like Nancy Drew still is, the heroine of the feminist children's novel plays a variety of roles, takes an active part in shaping her destiny, and does not relinquish her personal power. If she does not already know how to speak for herself, she learns in the course of the novel. If she does not already know how strong she is, she learns. If she does not already know how to combine the strengths traditionally associated with femininity with the strengths that have not been, she learns.

Many feminist children's novels seem to be direct revisions of earlier images of passive femininity in children's literature. Lissa Paul has demonstrated one example of this in "Enigma Variations: What Feminist Theory Knows about Children's Literature." In this article, Paul demonstrates how Margaret Mahy has rewritten the garden narrative of *The Secret Garden*, which signals defeat for the female protagonist, into a triumphant narrative for her in *The Changeover* (1984). Novels of fantasy and novels of realism have both been rewritten with such feminist scripts. The most noticeable feature of these revisions is the role the female protagonist often plays. She displays the characteristic willfulness of many of the girls in the so-called Golden Age of children's literature, but unlike heroines of earlier novels, she is not as likely to lose her self-possession. And in the process of maintaining her personal strength, she often subverts traditional gender roles, playing on stereotypes and stretching their limits by incorporating characteristics that are typically associated with both genders into her actions.

In some feminist novels such as Jean George's *Julie of the Wolves* (1972) and Robin McKinley's *The Blue Sword* (1982), when the protagonists lapse into the forms of earlier children's literature by becoming socialized in predictable ways in the final chapter, the endings of the novels seem unsatisfying because the reader has been unprepared for the protagonists' eleventh-hour decisions to conform to conventional expectations. More subtle novels like Nicholasa

Mohr's *Nilda* (1973) mask feminist agendas under ideologies that superficially appear to support the status quo of gender identity. And explicitly feminist novels like Cynthia Voigt's *On Fortune's Wheel* (1990) and Janet Lunn's *The Root Cellar* (1981) address openly the issue of gender indoctrination. What the novels I discuss in this chapter have in common is a clear textual effort to revise those traditional gender roles that mandate female submissiveness. Although these revisions take a variety of forms, most of them rely on a character who rejects stereotypical behavior to balance assertiveness with compassion. As a result, the character may overcome her confusion about her sexual identity by learning a self-acceptance that is rooted in a rejection of historical gender mores.

REVISIONS IN OTHER WORLDS

The success of Voigt's *On Fortune's Wheel* as a feminist fantasy that revises gender roles is best understood in contrast to a more conflicted other-world fantasy, *The Blue Sword*. In the latter novel, McKinley appropriates the male hero-fantasy archetype for a female protagonist.[1] *The Blue Sword* is the story of Harry, a significantly masculinized nickname for "Angharad," and her quest to understand her own agency. Much like King Arthur's, Harry's quest involves her discovering her royal heritage and gaining the sword that gives her the strength to lead others in battle. As for the text's ideology, while the narrative explicitly critiques the colonization of various cultural groups, the text seems unaware that it sometimes inadvertently and uncritically demonstrates men colonizing women. For example, only four of the king's fifteen knights (or "Riders") are women, and they remain unnamed.

Despite such flaws, *The Blue Sword* is a conscious effort at creating androgynized fantasy; that is, McKinley is clearly trying to revise gender stereotypes. The heroine with the masculine name is discontented in her gender-restricted role as orphaned younger sister of a military adjutant stationed at an outpost of the "Homeland." Harry and one of the compound's officers, Colonel Dedham, love the desert and the surrounding hills of Damar, unlike most people stationed at the outpost. Harry and Dedham also respect the Damarian ruler,

King Corlath, who comes from the hills seeking an alliance against the evil, nonhuman forces amassing under the wizard Thurra in the North. Corlath ends up kidnapping Harry because of what he later recognizes as her *kelar*, her magical powers that include the ability to foresee the future and to communicate with ancient spirits. Corlath notes that the gift of *kelar* is now used only as a battle tool, but it "was once good for other things: healing and calming and taming" (37). In other words, *kelar* once had more intricate uses than it does in Corlath's day, when it is regarded almost entirely as a male prerogative used to wage war. Harry's possessing it, however, implies that it can regain its former complexity.

Harry gradually comes to recognize and control her *kelar*. At one point she drinks a strong spirit that helps her foresee the battle they must fight with the Northerners. In the resulting vision, she perceives the leader to be a man; only later does she recognize that she herself is that leader. Thus, she eventually becomes what was for her initially unthinkable. As she develops into a war leader, she engages in a variety of activities that no female at the Homeland outpost would participate in: she learns to ride a battlehorse without stirrup or bridle as the Damarians do; she wins the jousting tournament to become the champion fighter and a member of the king's elite Riders; and he gives her the Blue Sword, Gonturan, always referred to with the feminine pronoun and said to have been passed down from the greatest queen of all, Aerin, through the women in Corlath's family. With the physical and mental strength Harry develops during her trials, she eventually unifies the tribes of the Hillfolk and leads them in battle to defeat the Northerners. Even some of the Homelanders eventually join the battle, and Harry is leader of them all. Harry's victory is both political and social; she has demonstrated to the people of her culture that women can be leaders.

Unfortunately, Harry's speech is often silenced throughout the text. Because she has been kidnapped by people who speak a foreign language, she must learn the language of those who have colonized her. And although when she experiences her visions she speaks in the Old Language, she must rely on Corlath to interpret for her, for she does not understand that language when she is conscious. Such linguistic choices as these partially limit Harry and make the final

chapter of the book seem at times stilted. For example, after spending the length of the novel becoming friends and conversing like
normal people (albeit, with the male dominating almost every conversation), Corlath and Harry lapse into the forced language of high
romantic fantasy as they verbalize their love for each other. They discuss wearing each other's sashes, which would be a mark of betrothal, in language that turns what might have been a touching tribute between two equals discovering their shared feelings into a
maudlin oration:

> Harry said clearly, that all might hear: "My king, I would far
> rather you kept my sash as you have kept it for me in faith while I
> was gone away from you, and gave me your sash to wear in its place.
> For my honor, and more than my honor, has been yours for months
> past, but I saw no more clearly than did you till I had parted from
> you, and knew then what it would cost me if I could not return.
> And more, I knew what it would cost me if I returned only to be
> a king's Rider." (258)

This speech demonstrates a central problem feminists face: the marriage plot often signals an ending of the heroine's independent ways.
Here, Harry's stilted language signifies that she must continue giving
up her natural voice if she is to marry Corlath.

The novel is an important one for feminist children's literature,
however, for it rewrites the hero quest with a female protagonist.
Moreover, two other women, one a girl Harry defeats in the tourna-
ments and the other the leader of a tribe of archers, have special
bonds with Harry because of her gender, and Harry's spiritual mentor is Queen Aerin. Although these three women make a limited
number of appearances in the text, especially when compared to the
large number of men who serve as mentors and friends for Harry,
the text does present at least some semblance of sisterhood. At the
end of the novel, Harry relies on some of the strengths stereotypically associated with femininity to reunite the Hillfolk and the Homelanders; without the value she places on connectedness within relationships and her ability to communicate about them, peace could
never be achieved. Harry also gives birth to four children who will

presumably cultivate the less gender restricted and less colonized world that she has helped to create. Femininity in this novel at least tries to be many-faceted.

Cynthia Voigt's *On Fortune's Wheel* is another self-conscious and far more successful attempt at claiming the male hero quest for feminism. Like Harry in *The Blue Sword*, Birle journeys into a foreign land with a man, Orien, who is a member of the royalty, but unlike Harry, Birle does not give up her voice, her identity, or her culture when she marries Orien. Birle begins her journey accidentally. She is not passively kidnapped; she falls into the river trying to rescue her family's boat as Orien is stealing it. She serves as his guide for a while and then decides to join him on his journey in the hopes of escaping an unwise betrothal she has made. She has also fallen in love with Orien, so she chooses to be with him. Setting the narrative apart from many fantasy quests, the characters in *On Fortune's Wheel* do not seek some specific object, nor do they seek to defeat a specific foe. Instead, it is the process of the journey, which allows the characters' love for each other to grow, and not the end of the journey that matters. This narrative choice more than any other separates *On Fortune's Wheel* from the traditional hero quest.

Imagery of cycles and wheels informs the text to emphasize how Birle and Orien's journey is process- rather than goal-oriented. The philosopher who buys Birle after she is sold into slavery tells her, "There are some . . . who say that the Lady Fortune has a wheel, and all men are fixed upon it. The wheel turns, and the men rise, or fall, with the turning of the wheel" (193). (The philosopher's gender-specific language is a mark of the culture in which he lives. This feminist novel is by no means free of sexist characters.) After Birle and Orien return to the earldom where Orien is heir apparent, Birle tells the earl that Orien has been "a slave to ill fortune, and now he is—again—Fortune's favorite" (252). The earl later echoes Birle's Boethian philosopher, noting that "the year turns on a wheel, like Fortune's wheel" (255). Birle and Orien's journey is even roughly circular in shape, beginning at the Falcon's Wing Inn, where Birle's family has their holding, and ending in the same area. This narrative movement so common to children's novels here underscores the text's emphasis on circularity and process.

The image of people being held captive on the wheel of fortune is paralleled by the text's puppet imagery. Birle and the giant Yul, who is her fellow slave, are entertained by puppets in the market square. Later, at a festival of the whole town, they are again entranced by puppets, and Birle perceives the queen who presides over this festival as a puppet herself. The queen, "for all her high birth and riches, was no different from Birle. She too had her life determined by the desires of others, and she too stood at peril" (174). When Birle and Orien return to the court where Orien's grandfather is earl, Birle feels "as if she were a puppet on a stage, being presented before the people of the castle, who observed from their places in the audience how the doll performed" (247). And at the end of the novel, when Orien chooses to give up his earldom, he decides to become a puppeteer.

Birle, however, eventually rejects this notion of being a puppet, so she also ultimately quits thinking of herself as trapped on fortune's wheel. Unhappy with life at court, Birle leaves Orien and sets up a holding where she can raise their daughter and use what she has learned from the philosopher to become a healer. Birle's unhappiness at court is expressed in fairy-tale terms; she has been a sort of Cinderella who has gone from serving as her bourgeois stepmother's servant to living as the heir apparent's chosen in the castle. The motif is almost comically emphasized when the shoes she is brought to wear in the castle do not fit her because they are too big. Rejecting this stifling culture, Birle returns to her own holding. Her stepmother criticizes Birle for not accepting "the way things are" and for wanting to change her life, to which Birle replies, "Why shouldn't things change, why should things always stay exactly the way they always were?" (259–60). When Orien comes to her holding and tells her he has given up his earldom for her and that he wishes to become a puppeteer, she thinks:

> Orien stood before her with their life in his hands to give her, and Birle . . . could think only of herself. What of her own life? What of her own work? What of the years she had thought to live with her daughter, the two of them, on the little holding distant from all the rest of the world. Must she give that up?
>
> Birle could have laughed at herself. She had gone beyond a place where the world could tell her *must*. Aye, and they both had.

Whatever Orien's work, she would grow the herbs and prepare the medicines, she would be herself and his wife too, and the mother to Lyss and whatever other children they had. She would be each of these, in the same way that Orien would be each of his puppets. . . . Her life was in her own hands. (275)

Birle does not give up her life to live as royalty in a foreign world as Harry does in *The Blue Sword*, nor does she need to forsake her love and live without him, as Elana does in Sylvia Engdahl's *Enchantress from the Stars* (1970). Instead, Orien makes the sacrifice for Birle while she simultaneously recognizes her own agency.

The issue of Orien's royal identity provides a consistent foil for Birle's similar quest. While Birle chafes against the narrowness of being female in this feudal society, Orien questions the entire premise of the feudal society. Rejecting his patrimony, he bitterly tells Birle that knowing who one's father is does not matter: "I know my fathers, for generations past" (41). He wonders why patrimony exists and why classes even exist, what gives one set of people the right to rule another, and why women are as disfranchised as they are. These questions lead Orien to run away in the first place; he doubts that a ruler who questions so much will make a good earl. But although the questing prince is an archetype who has filled the pages of literature since Odysseus sailed from Ilion, the story never becomes Orien's. Birle's strength and her growing recognition of it are the far more important story; Orien's story is the complement that completes Birle's narrative.

Early in the narrative, Orien tells Birle that she may come with him because "it's what I've been bred to do, rescue maidens in distress. From fierce dragons . . . or evil guardians, or wicked witches" (34). Yet from the start, it is never entirely Orien who rescues Birle, nor is it she who rescues him. Instead they help each other, save each other's lives, and serve each other as companions, as equals. Voigt has a clear agenda: she has set the story in this feudal society to illustrate how archaic our own society is capable of being when it perpetuates ancient, socially inscribed gender roles. And Voigt makes clear that she perceives equality and companionship between the sexes as the only possible way to reform that which in our own society is still feudal.

REVISIONS OF OUR WORLD

An early effort to revise children's realism of its sexism is Jean George's *Julie of the Wolves*. The story is a feminist Robinsonnade about Miyax, an Eskimo girl whose English name is Julie. At thirteen, Miyax has married Daniel, a mentally handicapped boy, in an arranged marriage. After Daniel tries to rape her, she runs away because she fears that no one in the conservative Eskimo community will support her. She plans to go live with Amy, her pen pal in San Francisco. A line in one of Amy's letters is the book's most explicit expression of its agenda to reform stereotypes; the California girl tells Miyax: "*I take dancing lessons, which I love, and I also like to play baseball with the kids that live on our hill*" (87). Amy confesses that she is proud of her big feet despite her mother's embarrassment about them because they help her climb and swim.

On her way to Amy's, Miyax gets lost in the tundra of Alaska and survives only because she learns to communicate with a pack of wolves. Amaroq, the leader of the wolves, becomes a surrogate father for her. She reclaims her Eskimo heritage, making herself a home out of sod and clothing from the hides the wolves have hunted. She, too, hunts; her first and most victorious meal consists of a stew she boils from an owl that she kills. The text describes with great detail and no sentimentality how Miyax must kill to remain alive herself, but her killing is always shown to be part of the ongoing life cycle that must continue if life is to be sustained on the tundra. For instance, Miyax observes how the seasonal disappearance of the rodentlike lemming allows the grass to grow long so that the caribou can graze; the wolves in turn hunt the caribou to keep them from overpopulating the tundra. The ideology embedded in these passages is explicitly ecological, but it contains an implicitly feminist message as well, for this ecological veneration of life cycles inherently praises the interconnectedness of life cycles that feminist texts so often embrace.

Rather than unfolding with the linear plot-line that is common in children's realism, *Julie of the Wolves* contains an embedded narrative structure that parallels the text's consciousness of cycles. Part 1, "Amaroq the wolf," describes Miyax's participation in the wolf community; part 2, "Miyax the girl," recounts her earlier childhood in Eskimo culture that led her to run away and join the wolf community;

and part 3, "Kapugen the hunter," describes what happens to Miyax after she leaves the wolf community. Nothing in Miyax's life happens in isolation, and nothing occurs in a straight line. Instead, she moves forward, makes mistakes, and moves forward again. Thus, the narrative structure parallels the nonlinear nature of Miyax's life and the cyclical nature of the novel's setting.

As for the cycles of the female body, the text openly addresses how a teenager living in isolation deals with menstruation by clearly stating that she has not yet reached menarche. Such an open declaration provides a positive contrast to another book of the same era that borders on using menstruation to titillate the reader: Judy Blume's *Are You There, God? It's Me, Margaret* (1970). In *Julie of the Wolves* menstruation is just another normal and not particularly remarkable aspect of the life cycle. *On Fortune's Wheel* contains the same calm acceptance of menstruation.

As winter nears, Miyax decides to return to civilization. The wolves follow her on her trek, and Amaroq eventually gets shot by hunters shooting from an airplane that Miyax later suspects belongs to her father. Miyax grieves the loss of her surrogate father deeply. That he has possibly been shot by her now-Americanized father shows that Miyax has been living in a gap between two cultures: she grieves for Amaroq far more than she has ever grieved for her father, Kapugen. After the slaughter of her beloved wolf-father, Miyax realizes she could never be happy living in the pink bedroom Amy has promised is awaiting her in San Francisco. Amaroq has been brutally shot for sport, and "in that instant she saw great cities, bridges, radios, school books. She saw the pink room, long highways, TV sets, telephones, and electric lights. Black exhaust enveloped her, and civilization became this monster that snarled across the sky" (141).

Miyax learns from a hunter's wife that her father is now living in a remote Eskimo village. She fantasizes that she can go live with him, and the two of them can "live as they were meant to live—with the cold and the birds and the beasts" (161). When she reaches the village and discovers how westernized her father has become, she thinks, "Kapugen, after all, was dead to her" (169). Taking her pet bird, a plover who was too weak to make the flight south for the winter but whom she has nursed back to health, Miyax sets out to return to the tundra where she can live in harmony with the natural world. But the bird dies, and Miyax suddenly recognizes her own frailty. She, too, is a bird living in the wrong environment; she, too, is vulnerable to the elements without others of her own kind to form a community. Singing out to the spirit of Amaroq in English rather than in the Eskimo tongue she has used exclusively since she has been on the tundra, "Julie point[s] her boots toward Kapugen" (170). Julie, no longer Miyax, must immerse herself in the language of westerners if she is to survive. When she reverts to English, it is as if she has lost her voice forever.

This final sentence places *Julie of the Wolves* squarely in the tradition of women's literature. As Lissa Paul has pointed out, one of the differences between women's and children's novels is that women remain entrapped in women's novels while children are more likely to escape their entrapments ("Enigma Variations" 187–89). Miyax, now entrapped by Western culture as Julie, must return to her father's world to survive. Such a denouement is typical of early feminist children's novels; the strong, individualistic female who is aware of the power of the life cycle must return to live within a patriarchal world because she knows no better way.

Nicholasa Mohr's *Nilda* is the story of a Puerto Rican girl who also tries to escape the gender entrapment her culture forces onto girls. The primary source of Nilda's socialization is her mother. Mrs. Ramírez, Mami, often tells Nilda that she is no longer a child, that she is a *señorita*, and so should act with more decorum (197, 270). Mrs. Ramírez's idea of adult behavior primarily revolves around silence: Nilda should not talk back; Nilda should not question authority; Nilda should not voice her opinion. Mrs. Ramírez is also obsessed with controlling Nilda's sexuality. One of Mami's lengthy diatribes is worth repeating in full, for it encapsulates her definition of what it means to her to be a woman:

> You wanna be grown-up and fool around with boyfriends, eh? Let me warn you. If you think it is hard now, Nilda, with the welfare people, ah hah! You don't like charity; you wish we didn't have to take that kinda treatment, do you? Just get yourself in trouble with one of those lazy guys, those *títeres*. Go ahead, get a big belly. And he goes off with another woman and leaves you. Or if he stays and tries, what can he make? What kinda job can be [sic] get? When he

himself still has dirty underdrawers? Don't bother coming here for sympathy, Nilda, because you must go with your husband; that is your duty. Then he can order you around. You who complain about your brothers being bossy all the time, and about your rights! Some rights you're gonna get. Well, what you have here to complain about is nothing, Miss, because I am here to protect you. But you try that with one of those no-good bums! First one baby, then two, three, four, a whole bunch. Dios mío! I was stupid, Nilda. Ignorant! What did I know? I had no mother, only a mean stepmother who beat me. If I could have had your opportunity for school and your privileges, never—lo juro por mi madre—never in a million years would I have had so many kids. (189–90)

For Mrs. Ramírez, being a wife means being trapped and being a mother means sacrificing herself into annihilation.

Nilda's reaction to her mother's campaign of terror is to reject her femininity. She is bemused by one friend's prissy attempts to emulate Shirley Temple and horrified by another friend's romance that leads to an unwanted pregnancy. Nilda is glad she is "a tomboy. I'd rather be that than go with any of them dopey guys" (189). Nilda is happiest at camp, away from the gender-specific pressures of barrio life, and she prefers her secret life of drawing to a secret life of romance. In that, she is different from most of her friends. Her artwork is a means for her to express herself in a community that continually represses her, and her art also provides her with a way to reject the stereotypical role of *señorita* that terrifies her.

Sonia Nieto has criticized *Nilda* for its negative depiction of Puerto Rican women (7), but between Nilda's rejection of gender stereotypes and her mother's dying words, the text does speak to feminists of all races. On her deathbed, Mrs. Ramírez makes clear for Nilda why she has tried so hard to terrify her daughter about her sexuality. "Don't have a bunch of babies and lose your life," she tells her daughter (275). "I have no life of my own, Nilda. . . . I have never had a life of my own. . . . nothing that is really mine" (277). She admits that even if she were to recover she would still "live for the children I bore . . . and nothing more" (277). Mami also acknowledges that she once had a different sense of herself, that she once felt in control of her life. She admits to having had the type of exhilarating experience that Nilda gets from her drawing: "I remember a feeling I used to have when I was very young . . . it had only to do with me. Nobody else was included . . . just me, and I did exist so joyfully in that feeling; I was so nourished . . . thinking about it would make me so excited about life. . . . You know something? I don't even know what it was now" (277). Before Mami trapped herself into nurturing other people, she was capable of nurturing, nourishing, herself. With these words, Mami makes clear that her agenda has not been to steep Nilda in the rigidly defined gender roles of 1940s Puerto Rican culture. Instead, she wants to liberate her daughter, to give her daughter something more than she has had. Toward that end, Mami has actually been fostering much of Nilda's rebellion all along. It is Mami who has sent Nilda to camp and Mami who, perceiving Nilda's emotional involvement with her infant nephew as too potentially a reproduction of mothering, disapproves of their relationship. It is Mami who sees to it that Nilda has the art supplies that provide her with one form of release from the gender roles traditional to Nilda's culture. Thus, Mrs. Ramírez provides the text with a double voice. Although her most strident voice is the one that counsels Nilda to act like a *señorita*, her more powerful voice is the one that counsels Nilda to reject the role.

At Mrs. Ramírez's funeral, Nilda hears her mother referred to as a Sleeping Beauty, as a Snow White entombed in her glass casket:

> "She was so young," said an older woman dressed in black.
> "Yes," added another woman, "and she looked so beautiful laid out in the coffin, just like in real life." (282)

In fact, in describing herself to her daughter as having no life, Mrs. Ramírez has made clear that she is the failed princess, the passive woman who in acting out societal expectations has essentially killed herself. But her death provides for her daughter's ability to reject the role of Sleeping Beauty. As the novel closes, Nilda has moved to her aunt's house, where she talks to her younger cousin Claudia. The girl provides Nilda with a sense of sisterhood that seems to help her overcome the initial stages of grief for her mother. Most important, Nilda shows her artwork to Claudia. Nilda's willingness to share her artwork with an admirer indicates that Nilda is coming into her own as an artist and that her salvation from her grief and from gender stereotypes lies in her using her artistic talent. The text is ideologically explicit in depicting the rejection of stereotypes as a weapon children can use against societal pressure to conform to traditional gender roles. In the way the text highlights how much the struggle for selfhood can be exacerbated by issues of heritage and ethnic identity, *Nilda* is especially significant as a feminist text.

A later feminist novel, Janet Lunn's *The Root Cellar*, which is written with a time-travel theme that allows the plot to unfold in two centuries, also rejects stereotypes as a source of female empowerment, but the text resolves itself with the more hopeful ending common to post-1970s feminist children's novels. *The Root Cellar* is written with a setting that could potentially be difficult for feminist revision, for part of the story occurs during the American Civil War. Many historical novels maintain feminist ideologies by showing how women could be strong within their own worlds; Patricia MacLachlan's *Sarah, Plain and Tall* (1985) and Katherine Paterson's *Lyddie* (1991) are motivated by such an ideology.[2] Sarah and Lyddie are more or less true to the gender roles determined by the times in which they were to have lived, so these books show strong females living within conventional gender roles. *The Root Cellar*, however, crosses gender by crossing genre.

Fusing together historical and speculative fiction, the conflict in *The Root Cellar* is triggered by a modern girl's being transported to Canada during the American Civil War whenever she enters her aunt's root cellar. Orphaned young, Rose Larkin must move in with relatives she initially despises. She seeks shelter in their root cellar and ends up in nineteenth-century Ontario wearing the jeans she had been wearing in the twentieth century, so the characters she meets, Susan and Will, initially assume she is male. After awhile, she does clarify her gender, but when she and Susan decide to find Will after he has been made a prisoner of war, Rose uses her friends' initial confusion about her gender to inspire her to masquerade as a boy. As Susan puts it, "Boys get paid more mind to" (100).

Throughout *The Root Cellar*, then, the nineteenth-century character, Susan, never acts outside of her prescribed gender role, but the twentieth-century girl, Rose, freed by the efforts of a century's worth of feminists, does. Rose works as a blacksmith's apprentice to raise funds for them to take the train to the hospital in Washington where they think Will is, and they do eventually find him. When they discover that he is near-crazed with despair over the death of his best friend, Rose and Susan work together to help the young man heal. Rose especially pressures Will when she tells him he has to get better because "I'm sick of being a twelve-year-old boy. I want to be myself, ordinary Rose. . . . I don't belong here. I thought I did but I don't— any more than you belong in the United States. I want to go home to Hawthorn Bay" (195). Rose, Will, and Susan all return to the place where they belong, but Rose has learned to be stronger and more accepting in the process.

Part of Rose's strength has come from discovering the strength within her own character: anyone capable of working as a blacksmith and surviving a long journey in another century is no weakling. Although she returns to the original world she once rejected (just as Miyax of the wolves must do), Rose does so with an increased acceptance of twentieth-century Canada. She wants to return to her aunt's world; she wants to be part of her cousins' lives. Since she knows she could choose to remain in the secondary world she has come to love, her choice to return to her original world is a triumph, not a defeat, for she has learned to respect it in a way that Miyax is never shown to have respected Americanized Alaska.

These characters, then, all take an active part in their own redemption. No knight in shining armor comes to save them; if anything, they save the knight. These female characters gain their strength by rejecting stereotypical expectations that girls must be submissive and by exploring their own choices. And in their decision making, each of them confronts a central truth about her gender: being female can give her strength.

Over twenty years ago, Carolyn Heilbrun celebrated literary androgyny as a force with liberating potential: "Androgyny suggests a spirit of reconciliation between the sexes; it suggests, further, a full range of experience open to individuals who may, as women, be aggressive, as men, tender; it suggests a spectrum upon which human beings choose their places without regard to propriety or custom" (*Toward* x–xi). Although Heilbrun's definition of androgyny rests solidly in entrenched stereotypes of female compassion and male aggression, her work was an attempt to free people from feeling confined by those stereotypes. And in feminist children's and adolescent novels, androgyny has proven to have been the type of liberating force that Heilbrun hoped it would be. McKinley, Voigt, George, Mohr, and Lunn have developed literary characters who enact power that is ultimately not necessarily gender specific.

Often in feminist children's novels, androgyny is used to indicate balanced power. Perry Nodelman praises novels that do "not so much blend male and female into genderless androgyny as [those that salvage] both masculinity and femininity as traditionally understood, and [keep] both intact and in battle with each other within the hearts and minds of characters of both genders" ("Children's Literature" 34). Although Nodelman rejects the term *androgyny*, his notion of the "paradoxical insistence" of incorporating the best of both genders seems to me to be the pinnacle of androgyny. The term does not necessarily mean something that is somehow desexualized as much as it illustrates the paradox of unifying both stereotypically masculine and feminine characteristics into a balanced whole.

Heilbrun calls androgyny necessary to an improved world order: "So long as we continue to believe the 'feminine' qualities of gentleness, lovingness, and the counting of cost in human rather than national or property terms are out of place among rulers, we can look forward to continued self-brutalization and perhaps even to self-destruction" (*Toward* xvi). Heilbrun is aware, as am I, that calls for androgyny tend to cast traditional masculine values as negative and feminine ones as positive, but for most feminist children's novelists, both genders have good and bad traits. Successful feminist characters are those who adopt the best traits of both genders to strengthen themselves personally and within their communities.

3.   SUBJECTIVITY AS A

GENDER ISSUE: METAPHORS

AND INTERTEXTUALITY

One of the most fundamental concepts to an understanding of poststructural feminist theory is that of *subjectivity*. Poststructural critics use the concept of subjectivity to question the liberal humanist position that the individual's inner self is the ultimate source of meaning (Belsey, *Critical Practice* 3). Different from the concept of "identity" often used in the study of children's literature, which implies that an individual has one fixed inner essence that makes her unique from all other people, subjectivity is a fluid concept based more on the primacy of language than on the primacy of the individual mind. Poststructural critics define the subject as constructed by language and by the exterior forces that language asserts upon the individual (Belsey, "Constructing the Subject" 46–50). Thus, it is language that makes us who we are.

The French psychoanalytic literary critic Jacques Lacan, for example, states that the unconscious mind is constructed like a language (*Four Fundamental Concepts* 149).[1] According to Lacan, language is the sole determinant of being: "The unconscious is that which, by speaking, determines the subject as being" (Lacan, *Feminine Sexuality* 165).[2] If having some form of language is what makes humans human, then we can say that they are socially constructed by language.

It is not so much that people manipulate language as it is that language manipulates them.

The concept of subjectivity, then, implies that every individual is multiply constructed by a variety of sociolinguistic forces that act upon her or him. Because language and the institutions it represents are so fluid, any given individual can occupy simultaneously a number of subject positions, some of which can seem at times even contradictory. In fact, it would be more accurate, if stylistically awkward, to refer to any given child assuming her subject *positions*, since any subject position is implicitly constructed from a variety of differing positions. As Judith Butler reminds us, being female constitutes an entire range of subject positions that can never be stable or uniformly defined: "there is very little agreement after all on what it is that constitutes, or ought to constitute, the category of women" (1).

Nevertheless, studies of subjectivity acknowledge that language is fundamental to how women come to occupy various subject positions. Such a premise implies the primacy of language; without it, the individual would have no being. The subject is who she is because language has so fashioned her. She has been constructed, as we all have been, by the cultural forces of language that have acted upon us. Immersed in cultural forces as she is, the subject depends on language to define her very being.

Francis Jacques explains how subjectivity is a linguistic process that derives from and depends on the interactions inherent in human language activities. He formulates the thesis that subjects only develop a sense of self-identity if they are able to think of themselves in the first person, as *I*, in the second person, as *you*, and in the third person, as *he* or *she* (xv). In other words, subjectivity is determined by the individual's perception of herself in all three grammatical persons: the first person, the second person, and the third person.[3]

Jacques further notes that the use of the third person is not always the objectifying process that Emile Benveniste argues it is. If a person is linguistically situated in the object position of a sentence, she is not automatically objectified; she is not necessarily deprived of her humanity and transformed into an object devoid of agency (35). On the contrary, perceiving one's self from the third-person point of view allows for an unlimited range of possibilities that the first-person point of view alone might exclude. Distinguishing one's self from others in the process called "individuation" depends on the ability of the subject to perceive herself from a variety of positions. As Catherine Belsey puts it, "'Identity,' subjectivity, is thus a matrix of subject-positions, which may be inconsistent or even in contradiction with one another" ("Constructing the Subject" 48).

To refer to someone's "subject position(s)" is to acknowledge simultaneously her dependence on language structures and her point of view within the matrices of her subjectivity. "Taking the subject position" generally refers to an individual's situating herself in the first person and recognizing herself as the agent of an action; "the object position" would be the corresponding perception of one's self as the recipient of the action. Whoever is in the subject position is an actor, just as the person in the object position is a receiver, as is the case in any transitive verb sentence: Lee hugged Terry. Lee is the actor, the agent, while Terry is the recipient, the object of the action. We can say, then, that Lee is in the subject position and Terry in the object position. But when Lee recognizes her agency, she "takes" or "claims" the subject position.

For textual studies, subjectivity involves these two separate but related issues: who has agency in a text? and how has language shaped that subject's agency? Russian literary theorist Mikhail M. Bakhtin investigates the "dialogics" of a text: the competing dialogues which interact to construct the narrative's meaning (269–75). Feminist theorists have used Bakhtin's theory of dialogics as they investigate textual subjectivity. Dale Bauer, for example, explains Bakhtin's usefulness for feminists: "In reading, the feminist critic becomes double-voiced, engaging in dialogue *with* the text and reaffirming the debate of voices" (xiv). In chapter 2, when I discussed Mami's competing sexist and feminist voices in *Nilda*, I was employing feminist dialogics to analyze the text.

Another concern of many feminists has been the individual's perception of herself in the subject position: is a female character allowed agency? Some feminists also ask if the dialogics suppress or liberate the character's agency. And they want to know how the reader's and the critic's subjectivity is engaged by the written text. The same basic issues inform the study of children's literature when critics investigate whether or not a child character has resolved her own problems and what the effect might be on the child reader. A major criterion of the feminist children's novels, then, is the protagonist's capacity for assuming and retaining the subject position within the competing voices of the narrative. In children's literature, assuming the subject position is particularly important because children so often seem to lack agency within our culture. One of the most important functions of children's literature is to depict children who enact the agency that children in real life may not have. And since feminism is so often involved with examining who holds power within a given cultural context, the purposes of feminism and children's literature are easily united.[4]

The character Winnie Foster in Natalie Babbitt's *Tuck Everlasting* (1975) demonstrates the basic principles involved in investigating textual subjectivity. Initially self-absorbed, Winnie seems to focus only on her first-person self. But since she perceives herself as an object of parental authority, she is unaware that she holds a subject position. Winnie's sense of herself as object is illustrated after both her grandmother and her mother reprimand Winnie, and she tells the toad she befriends early in the narrative, "I'm tired of being looked at all the time. I want to be by myself for a change" (14). Winnie expresses her feeling of being in the object position with a visual metaphor; she is "tired of being looked at." She also expresses her desire to claim the subject position as something she can perceive happening only if she is alone. The novel charts Winnie's progression toward a full-blown recognition of her subjectivity that includes her ability to switch subject positions so that she can perceive herself from all three points of view: from the first, second, and third persons. And her increased awareness of her own subjectivity does not rely on her being alone; in fact, she experiences it as part of a community.

Winnie learns the secret of the Tuck family, that they have discovered a fountain of youth and so are immortal, so the Tucks kidnap Winnie and take her away from her restricted life. They treat her well, and Winnie grows to love them. At one point, as Winnie and the father of the family, Angus Tuck, float on the lake, Winnie begins to perceive herself in the second person, as the object of Tuck's "you." As Tuck explains how terrible it is to be stuck forever in time without being able to age and die, he tells her, "You, for instance. A child now, but someday a woman. And after that, moving on to make room for the new children" (63). Winnie thinks about this, "and all at once her mind was drowned with understanding of what he was saying. For she—yes, even she—would go out of the world willy-nilly someday. Just go out, like the flame of a candle, and no use protesting. It was a certainty" (63). She combines her ability to perceive herself as the second-person object of Tuck's conversation with her well-developed capacity to perceive herself as a third-person object when she recognizes that in her own future she will die. Her split subjectivity fuses, for she understands that the person whose death she is contemplating in the future is not someone else's; it is her own. When she tells Tuck, "I don't want to die" (63), she is realizing the completion of this fusion process. She is beginning to understand that she has a place in the life cycle and that part of her place is in interacting with other people.

But Winnie does not act on this newfound principle until she makes a self-sacrificing decision that demonstrates she can finally take her own subject position by thinking of a third-person party in the subject position. Winnie's ability to empathize with Tuck's wife, Mae, allows the girl to take Mae's place in jail after the woman has murdered a man who has discovered the Tucks' secret and wishes to exploit it. Actually disguising herself as Mae, Winnie assumes the woman's identity and takes on her subject position in a process that still leaves Winnie's own identity intact. She fools the jailer into thinking she is someone else during the night, but she cannot sleep the entire night, for she is fully aware that she is not Mae: "So she had lain there, pulse thudding, eyes wide open" (128). While feigning someone else's sleep, Winnie knows exactly who she is. She has defined her own agency by understanding and temporarily assuming someone else's subject position.

Kim Aippersbach notes that at the moment Winnie takes Mae's place, Winnie achieves the type of feminine maturity that Carol Gilligan defines as oriented toward building relationships (89). I take exception with Aippersbach, however, when she says that "Winnie's final ordeal is not to save herself; it is to save Mae Tuck and, by extension, the world. In taking Mae's place in jail, Winnie symbolically becomes another person, thus becoming more fully herself" (89). Winnie is saving herself, too, since she is part of the world, so although her act is self-sacrificing, it is not entirely selfless—nor should it be. The dialogics of the text allow Winnie to claim her subject position within a community.

Investigating textual subjectivity can take several forms, including noting how the dialogics of the text have enabled a character to perceive herself in more than one subject position, as the text of *Tuck Everlasting* exemplifies. Winnie has come to accept her subjectivity as a result of the competing dialogues in the novel that position her in the first, second, and third person. Another of the simplest forms that studies of subjectivity can take is to note the individual's perspective. Demonstrating how a child can change her point of view implies a certain type of power: the power of a more complete understanding of the world. Those who know how to look at things from a variety of angles are not restricted by the narrowness that a monolithic vision enforces. For example, in Patricia MacLachlan's *Arthur, for the Very First Time*, Arthur learns to perceive himself as both agent and object by metaphorically experiencing the differing visions that looking through both ends of a telescope affords.[5]

Feminist authors like MacLachlan also explore the nuances of subjectivity through their use of language. For example, visual metaphors and metaphors of photography lend themselves to explaining the difference between the subject and object, so many feminist children's novelists include such metaphors in their texts. Naming, as a linguistic practice that implies ownership, also calls attention to subjectivity. Someone self-named or who names other things displays more agency than whatever or whomever receives the name. Closely related to naming practices are birth images, for newborns require names. Birth imagery in feminist children's novels often serves as a metaphor for subjectivity: when the character discovers her sense of agency, she is essentially reborn. Exploring the metaphors of perspective, vision, photography, naming, and birth in such texts as Jean Little's *Look through My Window* (1970), Virginia Hamilton's *A White Romance* (1987), Patricia MacLachlan's *Journey* (1991), and Angela Johnson's *Toning the Sweep* (1993), then, can lead to an increased understanding of how subjects are textually constructed.

Finally, subjectivity can also be explored through an author's use of intertextuality. Intertextuality occurs when one text makes reference to a preexisting text, as, for example, *Little Women* does when it refers repeatedly to John Bunyan's *The Pilgrim's Progress* (1678). The result is a dialogic tension between the two texts, as one text comments on the other. Authors often revise the preexisting tale to suit their own purposes as they incorporate the older tale into the newer one. Feminist authors are especially likely to revise existing folktales to emphasize a character's subjectivity, as Virginia Hamilton does in *The Magical Adventures of Pretty Pearl* (1983), as Francesca Lia Block does in *Weetzie Bat* (1989), and as Margaret Mahy does in *The Tricksters* (1986).[6] A character's subjectivity can be defined in a number of ways, but investigating a text's metaphors and intertextual references are two approaches to understanding the process.

METAPHORS OF SUBJECTIVITY

The controlling metaphor of *Look through My Window* is self-evident in the title. Emily Blair learns to understand people who are different from herself as she learns to "look through [their] windows" (202, 224). The person whose perspective Emily best comes to understand is that of her friend Kate Bloomfield. The girls discover that they have religious differences, but that those differences don't matter nearly as much to them as their similarities do. Their chief similarity is their interest in writing. Both of the girls are budding poets. Emily describes one of her poems as "part of herself put on paper," so her self-perception is rooted in her dependence on language (154). She recognizes that her inner being is constructed by language because she knows that she can transfer that being onto paper with the words of her poem. In a poem early in the text, Emily contemplates her life and what she will do with herself while her parents are away:

> I'm always just
> The me they see—
> Not the real true
> Inside me.
>
> But now they're gone.
> I'm free, free, FREE!
> I'll be the real true
> Emily.

Emily then puzzles over what exactly the "real true" Emily is. She never actually articulates her self-definition, but clearly it is her inner life as a poet. She recognizes that her parents objectify her but intuitively knows that her subject position is an interior space.

The language of being either an insider or an outsider permeates the text. Emily does not feel like an insider with the "horde of children" she plays with in her apartment complex (8). And after her family moves into a house and she discovers a locked box containing poems written by two girls she hasn't met yet, she again feels excluded. But as she makes friends with them and begins to feel like an insider, she worries about making "Kate stop looking as though she felt like an outsider" (183). Kate's proclamation that Emily "understands me" is a high point for Emily; she has received validation that she is indeed capable of changing her own subject position, that is, of looking through her friend's window.

Looking through windows has not only a metaphorical meaning for the text; the novel also contains a bona fide voyeur, Mrs. Thurstone, the next-door neighbor who watches the Blair family through their window. Whenever they do something unexpected, Mrs. Thurstone rushes over to make sure they are all right. The family tolerates her spying with amusement because they recognize the concern that motivates her nosiness; they understand that Mrs. Thurstone's spying through their window is only her way of observing their lives with empathy.

The metaphor is a particularly visual one, as metaphors of understanding tend to be in our culture: to express our understanding of something, we talk about having a "point of view" or a "perception" or "seeing" what someone means. Visual metaphors emphasize the subject/object split: whoever "sees" is automatically in the subject position, as Mrs. Thurstone is, gazing at something which is in the object position. So for Emily to learn by "looking through people's windows" is for her to recognize her own subject position and for her then to be able to switch positions; by taking someone else's, she shifts her own subject position. The book ends with Emily thinking about the subject position of the baby her mother is about to have. She links the baby's birth, then, to her or his subjectivity; the baby will "look through windows" as surely as Emily has, so the baby serves also as a metaphor for Emily's new self-understanding.

Virginia Hamilton's *A White Romance* deals specifically with the way a young girl learns to claim the subject position within a heterosexual romance. In that sense, *A White Romance* is a revisionist text because it ultimately does not allow for the traditional silencing of a female in a love relationship. Since the female character, Talley, is black and her tyrannical lover, David, is white, the text communicates ideologies of race as well as gender: oppression of African Americans, oppression of women, and oppression of African American women are all three overcome when Talley claims her subjectivity by rejecting the object position into which David has forced her.

Talley is a long-distance runner who has named two of her white friends "A White Romance" because their passion for each other is so blinding. The name communicates how she feels like an outsider and different from them; they have something she does not have: romance. She continues to call the couple "A White Romance," even though it embarrasses them, for the name is a way for her to assert authority, to claim some sort of agency. Then she creates a different sort of white romance for herself in a relationship where she is an insider when she falls in love with David. Dating him is a way to rebel against her father's strictness, but for a long time Talley doesn't see that she has traded one male's repression for another. David objectifies all women, giving "them the once-over" (106), and he tries to possess Talley by telling her that her black friend Victor wants to own her himself (111). David is a drug dealer, so his transforming Talley into a commodity seems no surprise. He gets furious with her when she tries to set boundaries about her body and her sexuality; three times he tells her, "Don't tell me don't" (121–22). David sets the time and place of their meetings; David tells her to whom she can and cannot talk. Talley even quits running. Eventually, Talley comes to think of herself as "chained" (134). She thinks, "Her goose was cooked. She was a dead, plucked ducky. Wasn't nothing she could do. She was in love. She loved him so. Love had taken hold of all of her. This was love? . . . Tears filled her eyes all the time" (136). She despises herself (138).

Talley doesn't free herself from this objectifying relationship until she goes with David to a Judas Priest concert. There, she perceives everyone in the audience as objectified. She herself cannot move; she is pinned in place by the crowd even when she needs to vomit. The demoralization of the heavy metal concert makes Talley realize she is worth more to herself than this. When David tells her, "As long as you are in my house at your own free will, you belong to *me*," she is stunned (176). "Always, she'd wanted him to say she belonged to him. But now, she was shocked to hear him say it the way he had. I belong to myself, she thought" (176). Although she cannot yet articulate her sense of self to David, she does accept that their relationship objectifies her. She apologizes to her friends for calling them "A White Romance" and tells them, "You have a right to be who you want to be. And I want you to know, you . . . are better than any white, black, or green romance" (189). Talley finally considers dating Victor, who has recognized her individual worth all along. She likes the choices Victor gives her (188), and to mark her reclamation of her agency, she starts running again. She especially likes that Victor runs with her in a noncompetitive way. The narrative closes, "No way was she going to pass him. But she stayed with him, clear to the bus stop, not *even* a pace behind him" (191). Talley has learned to engage her agency even when a male she loves doesn't want her to, and she has learned this entirely from the dialogues she has been immersed in with David, with Victor, and with her other friends.

MacLachlan's novel *Journey* is a feminist text that explores an adolescent male's subjectivity. The story is about an eleven-year-old named Journey by his nomadic mother. Journey and his sister live on their grandparents' farm because first their father and then their mother left. Journey is unwilling to admit his anger at his mother for abandoning him; he is more comfortable with being angry at her for ripping up all the family photographs before she left. His sister calls the destruction a "murder" (49). Journey's grandfather tries to replace the pictures by taking new ones, so photography is the central metaphor that controls both the events of the story and its narrative structure.

Photography helps Journey come to terms with his anger. Initially, he hates his grandfather's incessant photographing. The boy's frustration with his mother and with his grandfather coincides when Journey and his sister receive mail from their mother. Their grandparents warn them that there will be "money in that envelope. Not words," but Journey is still disappointed when this proves to be the case (7). He points out to his grandfather that their mother has attached to the money pieces of paper that have their names on them: "There are words! Our names are there. Our names are words!" (8). Journey recognizes the importance of names in claiming one's subjectivity; nevertheless, he feels victimized. So when his grandfather immediately begins to take a picture of him, the reinforcement of his position as an object angers him: "I stood, suddenly angry, wanting him to stop taking pictures" (9). Journey means that he wants to feel a sense of agency.

Just as Emily has recognized her subjectivity through the art of writing poetry, Journey eventually learns to assume agency in his life by means of his chosen art: photography. That he is the first-person narrator of his own story hints at his burgeoning sense that artistic creativity is a method of subject formation, but his greatest transformation occurs because of photography. He begins to use his grandfather's camera to take pictures himself. The more he takes on the role of the photographing subject, the less he rebels against being the photographed object of his grandfather's pictures. And the more pictures he takes, the more he can perceive himself as being like his grandfather. As Journey scrutinizes different photos, he also recognizes the physical resemblance to his grandfather that he has initially denied. Eventually, the camera leads him to acknowledge that the fond memories he has had of his father's playing with him are actually memories of his grandfather's playing with him. Journey has romanticized his father and so has refused to acknowledge his grandfather's involvement in parenting him. Once Journey perceives himself on both sides of the camera, he is able to embrace his grandfather's love. He accepts the relationship as one wherein his subjectivity is affirmed and he can both give and receive.

Birth imagery contributes metaphorically to Journey's understanding of his subjectivity when a stray cat wanders into the boy's bedroom. Breaking the family rule that one must not name an animal because once a person has named the animal, s/he has assumed responsibility for it, Grandfather dubs the cat "Bloom." (Journey's mother has broken the rule in a different way; she has named her children but has not assumed responsibility for them.) Bloom proves to be accurately named: she is pregnant. A connection between Bloom's and his mother's maternity is very clear to Journey. He wonders, "Who taught [Bloom] . . . how to be a mother," and when his grandmother answers that "mothers know," he replies, "Not all of them" (59). Journey worries that the cat will desert her kittens, as his mother has deserted him (63).

The cat gives birth to her litter in the ripped-up box of pictures that Journey's mother has left behind. The pictures in the box are ruined, but Journey seems ready to let the fragmented pictures go because an act of maternity has supplanted them. Thus, by the end of the story, Journey recognizes his subjectivity; he acknowledges his interrelationship with other people, and a metaphorical "murder" is replaced by an actual birth. Most important, Journey comes to terms with being abandoned because he can perceive himself as both subject *and* object.

In Angela Johnson's *Toning the Sweep*, the first-person narrator, Emily, expresses her growing understanding of her identity by operating a video camera. As with the protagonists in MacLachlan's *Journey*, Francesca Lia Block's *Witch Baby* (1991), and Trudy Krisher's *Spite Fences* (1994), the visual process of operating a camera creates a metaphorical experience during which the adolescent protagonist of *Toning the Sweep* comes to perceive herself as both subject and object. Emily and her mother have journeyed to the California desert to bring home Ola, Emily's grandmother, who is dying of cancer. On the trip to California, Emily's mother tells her about the journey she and her mother made when they moved to California in 1964. Emily thinks, "I wonder why she's decided to talk to me about all of that now. I can think of about a thousand things to talk about on a plane. Not dead people, though" (4). But dead people turn out to be pivotal to Emily's understanding of her own agency. Ola tells Emily that in the nineteenth century, people often had coffin photographs made to preserve the memory of family members who had died. Since Ola thinks that she would prefer to make videos of all her friends in the desert before she leaves, Emily volunteers to do the project. The woman who lends Emily the video camera tells her that using it is "like poetry and eating to me now. You let the camera become part of you. Like your head and your eyes. If the camera were to fall out of your hands, it should be like your head falling off in the middle of a conversation" (18–19). The camera does, in time, become an extension of Emily's brain.

For one thing, videotaping Ola's friends is a way Emily can reconcile herself to her grandmother's terminal disease. It is also a way for her to reconcile herself to the tension between her grandmother and her mother. Emily never understands her mother's anger at her own mother; Emily only knows that her mother "rages silently and bleeds inside" because her father was lynched by white racists in Alabama in 1964 (35). Emily thinks her mother blames her parents' "lack of attention to civil rights for my grandfather's death," so she assumes that is why her parents have taught her to be so politically and historically aware of racial issues (35). But in a videotaping session, she learns from one of Ola's friends that it was her mother when she was fourteen herself who first discovered her lynched father dead beside his new convertible with "UPPITY NIGGER" painted on the car's side (35, 79). After hearing this story, Emily watches the videos for the first time in an attempt to make sense of the whole work she has created. She decides she "like[s] the jerky movements on the first tapes" and doesn't want anyone to edit them. The videotape represents Emily's ability to see herself within a historical context, and she understands that history is not something that should be edited to look smooth, polished, and whole. Because of what Emily has learned through the camera's eyes, she finally understands her mother and grandmother's relationship, and she also better understands her own place within the civil rights movement.

Emily's friend David Two Starr has also taught her to pay respect to tribal customs. He has grown immeasurably from participating in a powwow with other members of his tribe. He tells her, "It was something, Emmie. It changed me, the powwow, I mean. It's hard to explain. It's your people around you—not like . . . well, you know. It's not like the people who raised me. They're important and I love them, but it's the ceremony. I found ceremony and ritual in Arizona" (94). Emily recognizes that her family needs to participate in an African American ritual, a ceremony of mourning for the dead, so she arranges for her mother to "tone the sweep." According to the tradition, when "someone died, a relative would get a hammer and hit a sweep, a kind of plow, to let everybody know. . . . you had to do it right after to ring the dead person's soul to heaven" (65). Emily decides that since no one in her family toned the sweep for her grandfather, he must be a restless soul still trying to enter heaven. Assuming a strong subject position, she takes her mother out into the desert, and together they hammer the sides of a metal water tower (the closest they can come to emulating the sound of a sweep in the middle of the desert) until they have released some of their rage and grief over the man's lynching. Emily has refused to claim victim status, and her active role in helping her mother grieve enables the woman, too, to forsake her sense of her own victimization. The two are then able to join the farewell party celebrating Ola's departure from her home. This party is another ritual to help the community grieve.

As the book closes, Emily thinks, "Mama used to say, 'Don't look back. It'll make you an easier person, able to live in this world'" (103). But Emily has learned how to look back in ways that strengthen her. From the competing dialogues embedded within her mother's story, her grandmother's story, her grandfather's story, and the stories of her grandmother's friends, Emily has learned to place herself within her community. She has reconciled herself to her crippling grief, and now she can look to the future as well and live with the type of dignity her grandmother has taught her.

Having recognized that some people are objectified and some people choose to focus on how they are objectified, Emily chooses to focus on her own sense of agency. For Emily, as for Journey, Talley, Emily Blair, and Winnie, experiencing the object position is essential to developing a sense of agency. The various metaphors that these texts employ emphasize how each character is a subject who is determined by language but who is capable of using language to take action.

INTERTEXTUALITY AND SUBJECTIVITY

Intertextuality often serves the purpose of underscoring theme in children's novels, especially themes about agency. Judy Abbott admires "Cinderella" and *Jane Eyre* in Jean Webster's *Daddy-Long-Legs* (1912) because she herself is living through the similar *Bildungsroman* pattern of the orphan discovering love. In S. E. Hinton's *The*

Outsiders (1967), Pony Boy quotes Robert Frost's poem "Nothing Gold Can Stay" to foreshadow Johnny's death; Johnny cannot live because he is too "golden," too good. John Stephens notes that intertextuality "often plays a major part in attempts to produce determinable meanings and to acculturate the audience" (*Language* 85–86). Thus, when feminist writers include intertextual references to folktales or mythology, they often rewrite these tales to suit their own ideological purposes.[7] The form these ideological revisions usually take is to depict how much more aware of her agency the protagonist is than are the characters in the tale the author is revising.

Virginia Hamilton's *The Magical Adventures of Pretty Pearl* is a revisioning specifically of the John Henry folktale and more generally of African American folklore. Hamilton has even identified her agenda as a feminist one: "I started out wanting to create heroines, heroic figures, female, on the order of John Henry, and that's how I came up with Mother Pearl and Pretty Pearl. They didn't exist in the folklore. There are no figures like that—there's only Harriet Tubman and Sojourner Truth. They were real people but there were no figures that did these feats" (Mikkelsen 394). Hamilton's feminist god is the "god chile" Pretty Pearl, who enters the world of humans because she is distressed at seeing Africans becoming enslaved. She asks permission for her journey from her brother "the best god," John de Conquer (6). He warns her, "You can't fool around de human bein's too long, else you commence actin' human youself" (9), and he decides to accompany her on her journey. After they have arrived in America, John de Conquer separates himself from his sister so that she can undergo the tests necessary for her to understand her own subjectivity.

After John has gone his own way, Pearl splits into two gods that clearly demonstrate how people have multiply situated subjectivities: the child, Pretty Pearl, and her mother-self, Mother Pearl. Pearl is able to split herself in two, the text implies, because each of us is capable of maintaining the position of both child and parent. Pretty Pearl, Mother Pearl, and their spirit friend Dwahro discover the Inside People, a communal group of freed slaves who live in harmony with their Cherokee neighbors. When the Inside People learn that white hunters and the railroads are encroaching on their territory, they decide to flee north. Amidst the community's tension about the move, Pretty Pearl begins to feel competitive with the leader of the Inside People's children, Josias, so she uses her John de Conquer root to scare him and the other children. As a result of using her spiritual magic to hurt other people, she slowly loses her divinity, and her subjectivity becomes, for the first time, limited. One of the most immediate consequences for Pearl is her very painful separation from her subject position as Mother Pearl: "like Mother and me be separate, so. Like never before, thought Pretty. I don't know. Somethin' awful is goin' on and I did it" (207). Pearl's loss of her own maternal subject position borders on the tragic.

Of Hamilton's created gods, Mother Pearl carries the strongest message for feminists. She is the apotheosis of maternity, for she is maternity transformed into a divine being, but she fits neither of the stereotypes of black women that Nellie McKay identifies: Mother Pearl is neither the Virgin Mary nor the African American "mammy" (175). She is a caring, nurturing woman with strength, intelligence, and a sense of humor; she helps lead the Inside People on their trek to freedom. When they have arrived safely at their new home in southern Ohio, Mother Pearl whispers to her sleeping child-self, Pretty Pearl: "Oh yes, this be de saddest thing I do. For I must go home. De Conquer say so. You won't need the god-woman part to fit, not now" (292). Pearl returns to Mount Kenya, having grown to be a god after all. But she leaves her human child-self behind her in America to tell the story of the African gods to the Inside People.

Although Pretty Pearl barely remembers her mother-self and has no memory of ever having been a deity, she does remember her mother-self's stories, the stories of her own past. Her role in her new community is to be both storyteller and historian. She is the person who tells the Inside People of their connection to Africa, and her stories are the source of her cultural identity and of theirs. Thus, telling folktales becomes in this text a way for a female to claim her subjectivity. Only in the telling of folktales does Pretty Pearl retain a vestige of her former glory; only as the narrator of mythology can she resume her former subject position as god-child. Hamilton once said, "I think that when I did *Pretty Pearl*, it was the book feminists felt was a very feminist book" (Mikkelsen 396). Pretty Pearl and Mother Pearl are indeed strong women, but there is more to it than that. They are women who are strong enough to revise ancient archetypes.

They are female characters whose narrative existence critiques and rewrites mythological repressions of femininity into stories of transcendent female agency.

One of the most successful ideological revisions of the folktale tradition occurs in Francesca Lia Block's *Weetzie Bat*. The back cover of the paperback even capitalizes on the book's obvious fairy-tale structure, proclaiming, "Once upon a time there was a girl named Weetzie Bat." The book is set in Los Angeles, and much is made of the city's love affair with the fairy-tale world Hollywood creates both in the movies and in its own cultural climate. The core of the book's fairy-tale structure occurs when Weetzie rubs on a golden lamp and a genie comes out ready to grant her three wishes. The comedy of the scene relies on fairy-tale traditions, but it also creates a social commentary:

> "Greetings," said the man in an odd voice, a rich, dark purr.
> "Oh, shit!" Weetzie said.
> "I beg your pardon? Is that your wish?" (23)

Weetzie laughs and tells the genie that no, she wants to wish for world peace. The genie answers: "I'm sorry. . . . I can't grant that wish. It's out of my league. Besides, one of your world leaders would screw it up immediately" (23).

Weetzie then decides to outsmart the genie in a passage that is a commentary on fairy tales:

> "Okay," Weetzie said. "Then I wish for an infinite number of wishes!" As a kid she had vowed to wish for wishes if she ever encountered a genie or a fairy or one of those things. Those people in fairy tales never thought of that.
> "People in fairy tales wish for that all the time," the genie said. "They aren't stupid. It just isn't in the records because I can't grant that type of wish." (24)[8]

Weetzie then wishes for a boyfriend for her best friend, Dirk, a boyfriend for herself, and a house, which she expresses in her L.A. dialect: "I wish for a Duck for Dirk, and My Secret Agent Lover Man for me, and a beautiful little house for us to live in happily ever after" (24). The wishes all come true literally, in fairy-tale fashion: they do get a house; Dirk's boyfriend is named "Duck," and Weetzie's is named "My Secret Agent Lover Man," although he is sometimes called "Max."

The characters do not, however, live happily ever after, because although Los Angeles seems to be a fairy-tale setting, it is no fairy-tale city. The characters experience many of the ills of urban culture: alcoholism and drug addiction, discrimination based on race and sexual orientation, and the fear of AIDS and the grief of losing friends to the pandemic. At the end of the novel, Weetzie realizes that "they were all afraid. But love and disease are both like electricity.... They are always there—you can't see or smell or hear, touch, or taste them, but you know they are there like a current in the air. We can choose, Weetzie thought, we can choose to plug into the love current instead" (88).

Weetzie herself has chosen to "plug into the love current," asserting her subjectivity by exercising her own reproductive rights. When Max refuses to have a child with her, she has sex with Duck, Dirk, and Max so that when she gets pregnant, no one knows who the child's father is. My students often question Weetzie's ethics in betraying Max, but the text asserts that her choices about her body are hers alone and that no man has the right to decide for Weetzie what she will do with it. Block has revised the folktale of the fatherless baby in an attempt to communicate that part of Weetzie's subjectivity includes having agency over her own body. Whether or not the reader agrees with the text's controversial ideology, the reader can at least appreciate that Weetzie harbors no double standard, for when a baby appears on the doorstep whom Max has fathered with another woman, Weetzie adopts that child into their family.

The text of *Weetzie Bat* holds love and the connection of family and friends to be the only possible way to counterbalance the pain involved in twentieth-century life. The novel concludes: "I don't know about happily ever after ... but I know about happily, Weetzie Bat thought" (88). That is the text's highest feminist value: the primacy it places on the interconnectedness of human life and on the necessity of each person recognizing her or his subjectivity in order to maintain those ties. Thus, *Weetzie Bat* changes the ideologies of traditional fairy tales to affect social change.

Margaret Mahy also rewrites the folktale plot in a number of ways, but her revisions are as likely to address mythological narratives as they are fairy tales. *The Tricksters*, for example, concerns itself with effecting social change through the construction of family. Ariadne, called Harry, discovers that her father has had an illegitimate child by her older sister's best friend, so much of the narrative involves how the family learns to heal from the pain of this crisis. Paralleling the family crisis plot is a supernatural plot colored by fairy tales and classical allusions that describes Harry's process of claiming her own subjectivity. On the first page, the text evokes a folklore setting, for Carnival Hide, the summer house the family is vacationing in, is described as looking like a "magician's sign" (3). The house proves, indeed, to be a signifier of magic, for it is haunted. Harry even comments on the haunting, saying, "Something is waiting" (3).

Much like Emily in *Look through My Window*, Harry is a writer. She wishes for a book with magic powers that would make manifest each reader's agency. "As you read my book you alter the world. You read Chapter One, look up from its pages and—hey presto—things have changed" (23). She catalogs the changes that would occur as the reader reads her magic book: the world would get brighter, the moon would reproduce, mirrors would create rainbows, the people who live in mirrors would find their true selves, and "when you turned the last page, you'd find that you were a book yourself. . . . You were a book, and someone else was reading you. Story and real would take it turn and turn about, you see" (23). This intertextually powerful book that Harry envisions essentially becomes the plot of *The Tricksters*, for by writing a romance of "mysterious and threatening love" (13), Harry becomes the vehicle through which the ghosts can enter Carnival Hide (224). The ghosts are tricksters. They turn out to be three manifestations of Teddy Carnival, son of the original owner of Carnival Hide. That Teddy ends up having three ghosts metaphorically represents the multiple nature of subjectivity.

Classical allusions permeate the text. One of the ghosts, for example, is named Ovid after the Greek poet. Much more important in its implications for feminist revision, however, is Harry's real name, Ariadne. The thread that proves to be Ariadne/Harry's conduit is her storytelling. But unlike the original Ariadne, who gives her spool of thread to Theseus so that he can achieve the transcendence she never gains, Ariadne in *The Tricksters* uses her thread of storytelling to effect her own transcendence. Ariadne falls in love with the benevolent manifestation of Teddy's schizophrenic ghost, and because of the love she feels for him she gains a better sense of her own agency. Harry recognizes that the ghosts are physical embodiments that have been possible only because she has effectively conjured them up in her writing. Just as her namesake's thread provides Theseus with a conduit out of the labyrinth, Harry's tale spinning provides the ghosts with a conduit into reality. Although for a time she rejects her own writing because she is so scared of this power, by the end of the narrative she reclaims her subject position as a writer. In the final chapter, entitled "Once upon a Time," Harry decides to write again. As she stares at the blank page before her, she thinks, "The page was pure and certain, words were uncertain, but their uncertainty was what made them magical" (266). Harry understands that she can dialogically use words to create and to recreate: to create fiction, to re-create folktales so that they come out the way she wants them to, and to (re)create herself. Her sense of the power embedded in her ability to create represents the power inherent in recognizing her agency.

The text of *The Tricksters* exemplifies the intertextual use of mythology and folklore in feminist children's novels. It uses intertextual references to underscore its theme, but more important, when the original text oppresses females, the feminist author transforms the story, redeeming it from sexism and claiming it for feminism. Jack Zipes maintains, "Folk tales and fairy tales have always been dependent on customs, rituals, and values in the particular socialization process of a social system. They have always symbolically depicted the nature of power within a given society. Thus, they are strong indicators of the level of civilization, that is, the essential quality of a culture and social order" (67). That the ways a culture uses folktales reflect the culture's values seems clear. In rewriting folktales to advance feminist ideologies and to identify female subjectivity, feminist writers are both protesting the powerlessness of women inherent in our culture's old folkways and giving voice to a new set of values: a set that allows for the princess to have power, a set that allows Sleeping Beauty to wake up not to a destiny that immerses her in her husband's life but to a destiny that is self-defined.

The feminist triumph in all the narratives discussed in this chapter is the transcendence these characters display as they claim the subject position. They take the subject position as a way to grow and as a way to celebrate themselves, not as a way to have power over other people by putting them in the object position. All these characters are invested in their own subjectivity and in helping the people around them perceive themselves as subjects. Moreover, they develop their subjectivity dialogically, within the dialogues of the language that constructs them and within the narratives that intertextually interact with each other. The intertextual revisions and the language-driven tropes that permeate these texts—the visual metaphors, the photography metaphors, the naming metaphors, and the birth metaphors—are different ways of expressing how the construction of the subject works. The language and narratives that were once a means of repressing people become in these texts a way to liberate them.

4. TRANSFORMING FEMININE

SILENCE: PRO/CLAIMING

FEMALE VOICES

Literary proclamations of female subjectivity are important because too often throughout history, female voices have been silenced. Narratives that depict characters engaging their subjectivity, however, tend to focus on those same characters' articulateness. Such texts provide an important counterbalance to traditional depictions of female passivity. Some psychological theorists consider cultural silencing to be one of the dominant forces that shape female growth. For example, in *Meeting at the Crossroads*, a study that painfully delineates much of what causes psychological problems for women in our culture, Lyn Mikel Brown and Carol Gilligan describe the transformation of adolescent girls from being outspoken and confident at the age of eight or nine to being so concerned with being socially acceptable that they have learned to silence themselves by the age of thirteen or fourteen (4–6, 20–21).

Literary theorists have shown how this social phenomenon of silencing manifests itself in literature. In *The Madwoman in the Attic*, Sandra Gilbert and Susan Gubar identify aphasia, or speechlessness, as one of the defining literary metaphors of nineteenth-century feminine repression (58). The metaphor has certainly had an active life in twentieth-century women's narratives, as novels such as Margaret

Atwood's *The Handmaid's Tale* (1986) and films such as *The Piano* (1993) demonstrate. Elaine Showalter relies on feminists from Virginia Woolf to Adrienne Rich to demonstrate how "women have been denied the full resources of language and have been forced into silence, euphemism, or circumlocution" ("Feminist Criticism" 193).[1]

More germane to children's literature, Lissa Paul draws some literary parallels between the silencing of women and the silencing of children: "Children, like women, are lumped together as helpless and dependent; creatures to be kept away from the scene of the action, and who otherwise ought not to be seen or heard. But women make up more than half of the population of the world—and all of us once were children. It is almost inconceivable that women and children have been invisible and voiceless so long" ("Enigma Variations" 187). With this statement, Paul implicitly asks feminist critics to be sensitive to silencing as an issue in children's literature.

I will discuss in the following chapters how feminists have formulated interdependency as a narrative strategy through which females can overcome this socioliterary silencing. In this chapter, however, I focus on literary images of vocal repression and some of the ways female protagonists overcome that silencing in novels by three feminist writers for children: Mildred Taylor, Patricia MacLachlan, and Minfong Ho. The novels I address here display a number of textual paths to vocalization. For some characters, self-reliance and a refusal to silence their inner voices strengthen their public voices. For others, art provides a metaphorical expression of voice. Often characters recognize the dialogic nature of voice: their voices exist only in dialogues with other people. But whatever strategies lead to their recovery of voice, the feminist characters in these four novels ultimately gain an awareness of the primacy of language in defining themselves as subjects. They recover their voices because they recognize the power of language.

Regarding voice and silencing, Barbara Johnson writes about Janie, the protagonist of Zora Neale Hurston's *Their Eyes Were Watching God* (1937), that "aphasia, silence, the loss of the ability to speak" results when the woman is reduced to playing only one role (164). Johnson makes much of the "distinction between speech and aphasia, between silence and the capacity to articulate one's own voice" (164). Before Janie is capable of articulation, she must be able to recognize not only who she is but how she is different from those around her; her sense of self is dependent on her understanding of how her subjectivity is unique (164). But Janie cannot engage her agency until she articulates her voice.

The protagonist of another African American novel, Cassie in Mildred Taylor's *Let the Circle Be Unbroken* (1981), experiences much the same tension. She often experiences aphasia as a result of not completely understanding either her identity or her difference from other people within her community, rural Mississippi during the Depression. Throughout the Logan family chronicles, which include *Roll of Thunder, Hear My Cry* (1976) and *The Road to Memphis* (1990), Cassie is an articulate girl, almost always willing to voice her opinion. Yet the people around her often silence her. She confronts this experience in *Let the Circle Be Unbroken* and even comes to understand some of that silencing; it is the repression of the oppressed at the hands of the oppressor. The African American community in which she lives silences its girls as a result of being silenced by white southerners; they rightly fear what will happen to black girls who refuse to play the passive role in which white society casts them. For example, when Cassie's parents decide that she can go with them to support one of their elderly friends as she tries to register to vote, Cassie's mother tells her: "We decided you should go because it's important that you see this. But, Cassie, I expect you to keep that mouth of yours shut. I don't want to hear one word out of you all the while we're in that office, do you hear me? I'll do the talking" (353–54). Cassie agrees and keeps her promise because she understands the social dynamics that involve the silencing of an entire people. But although she is physically silent, she is not mentally so; she comments throughout the narration of her story on the events around her.

The silencing eleven-year-old Cassie does not understand, however, is her vocal repression at the hands of her fourteen-year-old brother, Stacey. Stacey often interrupts Cassie; in fact, he does so far more often than any other character in the book. The first time he does it, Cassie identifies it in her first-person narration as "an irritating habit he had recently picked up" (3). On the next page, she narrates: "Stacey cut me off. Again" (4). Stacey's control over Cassie's speech becomes even more aggressive as he gets more frustrated with his powerlessness in the face of segregation. When she complains that they cannot use the public wash facilities in the county courthouse, he interrupts her, "'Jus' hush up, Cassie. Hush up!' he snapped" (59). Feeling silenced by the white ruling class and fearing white repercussions against them, Stacey silences one of the only people around him who has even less power than he has: his little sister.

Equally frustrating to Cassie is her parents' willingness to listen to their son. When Stacey interrupts an adult conversation to ask about the upcoming trial of one of their friends, the adults answer his question. "I expected Mama and Papa to reproach Stacey for butting into so serious a conversation. Neither did" (39). The message is clear to Cassie: adults value her brother's voice more than they do hers. As a result of this enforced aphasia, Cassie eventually learns to silence herself around her brother. At one point, "Stacey looked away, trying to make up his mind. I started to say something, but decided I'd better not" (49). Later, Cassie decides not to tease her brother about his newly grown mustache: "upon Mama's advice, I wisely kept quiet" (208). Discretion here is the better part of valor; Cassie seems to be learning not only to repress her voice with white people but also with black males.

Truth, however, is always important to Cassie. She consoles herself that she knows the truth even if she cannot speak it. When she and her brother talk with a friend about his failing crops and Cassie utters the truth about them, her brother again interrupts her: "'Cassie, wouldja hush!'" (89). But Cassie's interior monologue reveals that her aphasia is only verbal, not mental: "I cut my eyes at Stacey and grew silent, not out of any resignation to his so-called authority but because I figured if he wanted to let Moe continue to delude himself about this sharecropping business, then that was up to him" (89).

One of the triumphs of the climax is Stacey's acceptance of Cassie's voice. After being released from an unwarranted incarceration in a Louisiana jail, Stacey actually asks Cassie to talk to him:

> "Cassie, how come you so quiet?" he said as he wiped his face.
> "You ain't gone and changed on me, have ya? . . . Or maybe you
> thinking . . . I'm the one changed. That's what you thinking?"

"Ain't you?" I accused. . . .

"Guess I have . . . but that ain't necessarily bad."

I looked at him warily.

"It ain't Cassie. Really. Why, if we don't change, things don't change, we might as well stay babies all the time. 'Cause when we grow, we bound to change. You eleven now, you oughta understand that."

"And I s'pose you do, huh?" I questioned, growing just a bit tired of his attitude of adult superiority. "You ain't grown yet, ya know."

He grinned at me. "Now you sounding more like Cassie." (388)

Cassie has never doubted her own voice nor has she doubted its validity, but the text's recognition that this male has been wrong to silence his sister affirms female voices in general and African American female voices specifically. For Cassie, part of accepting her identity seems to be recognizing the sources of her marginalization: she is a child, she is working class, she is black, and she is female; therefore, she must at times be silent against her will. But her narration reveals that her inner voice is never silenced and never will be, so her aphasia is never a complete one. Thus, Cassie transcends much of the societal silencing she has experienced by insisting on the legitimacy of her voice.

Those of Patricia MacLachlan's novels that focus on the development of preadolescent girls are similarly remarkable in the ways that they demonstrate girls gaining voices. The protagonists of *Cassie Binegar* and *Baby* (1993), for example, both overcome some form of adult-initiated silencing.[2] Central to these girls' discovery of voice is the value they learn to place on language. Until these preadolescents learn the power that language gives them, they feel frustrated and isolated. But eventually, they learn to rely on their inner capacity for using language to help them define their own subjective knowledge. They grow vocal when they learn to rely on their interior voices.[3]

MacLachlan's texts often articulate the protagonist's silencing by relying on the rhetorical device of aporia. According to classical rhetoric, aporia results from the impossibility of concluding an argument in which two contradictory statements seem either simultaneously true or simultaneously false (Kerferd 65). Because no conclusion can be drawn, the rhetorician is silenced. For example, one might feel perplexed, as does the protagonist of MacLachlan's *Unclaimed Treasures*, by the paradox that flying is both extraordinary and ordinary: for a human, flying is extraordinary; for a bird, it is ordinary (76–77). Given the original terms of the argument, however, no absolute conclusion can be reached as to whether the act of flying is itself purely ordinary or purely extraordinary. Plato resolves the paralyzing effect of this type of antilogical rhetoric with the implementation of a third term to create the conclusion of a dialectical argument: the synthesis. Unlike antilogic, the dialectic allows for the restating of the original question so that it can be answered (Kerferd 66–67). In this way, with the synthesis that intuitive thinking allows, the aporia that stems from binary thinking can be avoided.[4]

The concept of aporia is pertinent to MacLachlan's works in its metaphorical ability to demonstrate the centrality of language to a girl's subject position. While experiencing the aphasia of aporia, the individual cannot shape her own experience, nor can she interact with other people. She is only an object in other people's dialogues. Until MacLachlan's characters undergo a process that demonstrates how central language is both to their interior worlds and to their abilities to engage with the exterior world, they experience actual silences that metaphorically represent how powerless they feel within their own communities. But as MacLachlan's characters recover from their aporia, they develop a subject position that gives them new power. No longer silenced, no longer the object of someone else's experiences, they can finally engage with other people by expressing themselves. Their increased immersion in language processes, then, is instrumental to their growth.

In *Cassie Binegar* and *Baby* some form of artistic process serves as a metaphor for the character's immersion in language. For Cassie Binegar, the artistic process is barely metaphorical, since her mode of expression, poetry, is comprised entirely of words. The beginning of Cassie's sense of being silenced by the adult world manifests itself as writer's block when she has trouble finishing her poem "Spaces," which is about the physical spaces in which she seeks privacy. The reader may understand that Cassie is frustrated because she is too literal in her quest for a physical space in which she can feel good about herself, but the character must work through several aporic moments before she gains that knowledge for herself.

Cassie's first aporia results from a conversation with a voice of male authority, her older brother James. She says she wants her family to be "like everyone else" (16). James answers her by asking a rhetorical question: "And what is everyone else like, Cass?" (16). Cassie cannot answer him, so she retreats into herself after she tells him that he just does not understand (16).

Aporia again results after Cassie develops a crush on another male authority figure, Jason, simply because he is a writer. When Cassie asks, "Why don't I have a space of my own?" (69), she means the question quite literally; she wants an actual, concrete place where she can have privacy. But Jason answers her with a rhetorical question that denies the legitimacy of her question: "Each of us has a space of his own. We carry it around as close as skin, as private as our dreams. What makes you think you don't have your own, too?" (73).

Jason and Cassie are enacting aporia as a "semiological enigma" in the sense that Paul de Man defines it (10). Modifying the classical definition of the aporia to demonstrate how ambiguity influences textuality, de Man describes the tension that occurs when the answer to a rhetorical question negates the existence of the original question (9–13). An aporic silence invariably results from a rhetorical question when "it is impossible to decide by grammatical or other linguistic devices which of the two meanings (that can be entirely incompatible) prevails" (10). Thus, to the rhetorical question of a male authority which is notably couched in diction that denies the legitimacy of her original question, Cassie has no answer. She reinforces the silence she feels by turning out the light, "leaving herself and the questions in the dark" (73).

A later rhetorical question in a dialogue with her grandmother also silences Cassie. When she asks, "How come you don't see things the way they are?" Gran answers the literal question with a rhetorical question, "Tell me, just how are things? How *are* things?" (84). Again, Cassie is silenced; "No answers anywhere," she thinks (84). And because she feels bereft of language, she bursts into tears. But rather than leaving Cassie alone to work through her aporia as James and Jason have, Gran comforts the girl. In a brief story that relies on visual metaphors of subjectivity, Gran tells Cassie that her grandfather never did learn how to look through other people's eyes before he died. Gran shows the girl that her grandfather's rigid attempts to control the world around him kept him from enjoying his life (85). While reinforcing the matrilineal bond between them, Gran tries to teach Cassie to develop more than one internal perspective for judging things. In other words, a mother-figure uses a narrative to teach Cassie to shift her subject position. Because this process of adapting various subject positions can be accomplished more easily by someone who relies on her interior self to perceive theoretical possibilities than by someone who judges the world only in concrete terms, Cassie grows into a new stage of psychological maturity.

Once Cassie learns the process of recognizing shifts in her subject position, she gives up her quest to gain complete control over her environment and recovers her poetic voice. She finishes her poem "Spaces" by proclaiming that her mind is her favorite space. She describes her mind almost entirely in terms of language, for that is *"Where I sort out my thoughts and sighs / and shouts! / and cries"* (116). Having understood that the language of her thought processes is the only tool she has to exist peacefully in the world, Cassie concludes that the best space of all is her subjectivity, her mind: *"That is where I like to be / Because I know that's really me"* (116).

After Cassie comes to understand the power of her own thoughts, she recognizes that she is more in control of her life than she had previously realized. As a result, she is able to forgive her family (and especially her mother) for being disorganized. With the help of her grandmother, a matriarchal figure, Cassie has learned to embrace the powers of both her mind and her body, recovering both her interior and her exterior voice.[5]

The aphasia experienced by Larkin, the narrator of MacLachlan's *Baby*, is externally imposed on her by the authority of her parents. Like Cassie, she discovers an artistic process, in this case, dancing, that serves as a metaphor for the language process. This discovery enables her to overcome her conflict with her mother and her father. The conflict has arisen because a few months before the novel opens, Larkin's newborn brother died shortly after his birth. In the ensuing months, Larkin's parents have refused to talk about either the baby's death or his life, and their refusal has forced Larkin into a seemingly permanent silence. When Larkin's grandmother, Byrd, initially tries to articulate her sense of loss, the woman cuts herself off: "'But I do miss—' She stopped suddenly, and I looked at her, waiting for her to say what I knew she missed. What *I* missed" (9). The reader is herself placed in an aporic gap at this point since s/he still has not been told about the baby's death. The reader does not know what or whom the grandmother misses. That gap of undecidability continues when Larkin tells the reader everything has "changed because of what I was missing and no one would talk about" (18). The text itself still has not named the ineffable tragedy.

When Larkin finally does tell the reader at the end of the fourth chapter that she has been missing her baby brother, she reiterates the terms of her aphasia: "It was Mama and Papa I wanted to talk with, but Mama and Papa didn't talk. Not about this" (32). Thus, images of silence pervade the text. For example, on the first page of her narration, Larkin describes her father as "quiet and stubborn" all day at work; she contrasts this silence with the pleasurable sounds he makes in the evening when he tap-dances on the family's Italian marble coffee table (5). She cannot tap dance herself and wishes she could; but more important, she prefers the noisiness of her father's dancing to his silence. Later, Larkin is horrified when her mother cries silently: "There was no sound to her crying; only tears streaming down her face. I stared at Mama. *I had never seen Mama cry this way. Terrible, somehow, without the sound*" (21).

Larkin's mother has been crying silently because, in a fairy-tale plot twist, a destitute mother has abandoned her baby daughter, Sophie, at Larkin's home.[6] A year later, Sophie's mother returns for her daughter, but during that year, baby Sophie helps Larkin's family overcome the silent grief that has immobilized them since the death of their own baby. The text resonates with implications about the dynamics between silence and sound and about the power of words, names, poetry, and memory as functions of language.

When Larkin's mother decides they should teach Sophie new words, one of the central patterns in the book is reinforced. Words are important; they have tremendous power to affect self-expression, human interaction, and memory. The librarian at Larkin's school, Ms. Eunice Minifred, reinforces the theme by describing the power of words numerous times. Ms. Minifred starts the school year by telling the children: "This year we will be talking about the power of language. . . . The power of words. And how words can change you" (42). Ms. Minifred's speech causes Larkin to think, "What about when there are no words? . . . *Silence can change you, too, Ms. Minifred"* (42). As if Ms. Minifred were reading Larkin's thoughts, she goes on to say, "In this room, in these books, there is the power of a hundred hurricanes. Wondrous words" (43). That words are powerful and "wondrous" will be Ms. Minifred's refrain throughout the book. Ms. Minifred's students make fun of her belief in "the power of wondrous words" (58, 83), but her convictions invite the reader to pay attention to the importance of words in influencing people's experiences and interactions.

Larkin and her mother share a metaconversation about words when they discuss the ethics of their keeping Sophie:

> "We're doing the right thing." Mama sat back and looked at me. "You know that, don't you. Sometimes you have to do what is right."
> *What is right.* I didn't answer, but I felt my face grow hot with sudden anger. There were words in the spaces between us; those words we had never spoken, words about what *I* thought was right. It was hard to say what I thought without getting rid of those words first. Mama, staring at me as if she knew my thoughts, suddenly straightened her shoulders and went back to her drawing. Conversation was over, that one subject that stood between us closed. I watched her sketch, hating the look of her hand slipping across the paper as if she was brushing away all the words I needed to hear. (51)

The passage emphasizes the tangibility of words by casting them in almost physical terms with such phrases as "words in the spaces between us" and Larkin's inability to articulate herself "without getting rid of those words first" because of "that one subject that stood between us." Words, or the lack thereof, have an actual presence in Larkin's life. Not only is her communicative ability hampered by her parents' refusal to discuss their son's death, but the silence is beginning to affect Larkin's self-perception. Her statement that "it was hard to say what I thought" indicates that she is beginning to lose an understanding she had earlier of her own mental processes; she genuinely does not know what to think because she has not been allowed to speak. Moreover, she wants not only to speak but to listen, as the text makes clear when Larkin describes her mother "brushing

away all the words I needed to hear." Larkin intuitively acknowledges that a person-as-subject exists only dialogically when she expresses her desire both to speak and to listen. Once again, MacLachlan is stressing how subjectivity is defined by the language process.

A central metaphor for Larkin's horror at her parents' silence
comes from her inability to understand why they did not name their
infant son. This namelessness disturbs Larkin, for it makes the baby's
memory seem to exist in a vacuum. As often occurs in MacLachlan's
works, naming has primary importance as a way of determining a
being's subjectivity. Thus, the baby boy's namelessness reinforces his
lack of an existence, his lack of agency. Larkin tells her friend Lalo
that "they never named him" (52) and then is stunned when Lalo
suggests "*you* name him. . . . if you need him named, then you name
him" (54). Larkin reacts violently, telling Lalo he is "so dumb. The
very dumbest" (54). Her choice of adjective is a telling one: she is
obviously trying to cause him as much pain as he has caused her, but
the use of the word "dumb" sets up a strong contrast. Lalo, in fact, is
not dumb; it is Larkin who cannot speak.

Sophie's developing language skills serve as a contrapuntal foil to
Larkin's aphasia. The baby learns first words, then word games, then
sentences. Lalo says of Sophie, "She has all these words inside her, all
the things she's heard us say. She has *sentences* in her, sitting there,
waiting to come out" (75). This is as strong a statement as MacLachlan has ever made characterizing language as the shaping force of the
human subject. The language skills Sophie learns also solidify her
experiences at Larkin's home in her mind, for inserted throughout
the text are italicized passages narrated from Sophie's point of view.
But the reader can only guess the identity of the narrator of these
passages, for only at the end is the reader's guess confirmed that
these remembrances belong to Sophie. One of these memory passages focuses entirely on language:

> She remembered voices. And words like whispers in her ear. Words like
> the soft wind, touching her.
> Words. (78)

Without words with which to fashion these memories, Sophie would
not have them at all.

When Lalo suggests teaching Sophie poetry, Larkin objects because poetry is "Words. Just words" (75). But her father agrees with Lalo, rejecting Larkin's dismissal of poetry: "'Poetry?' Papa said softly. 'Just words?'"; then he looks at his wife and recites a line from an Elizabeth Barrett Browning love sonnet (75). The love he displays in reciting the sonnet shows how wrong Larkin has been. When Larkin discovers that her father has been reading Edna St. Vincent Millay's "Dirge without Music," the girl begins to understand the power of poetry to provide the reader with an emotional outlet. Learning that her father has received a solace from this poem that he has not shared with her enrages Larkin. "How could he have read this and not told me? All the months of *silence*. . . . How could he?" (89). The anger she feels at being so isolated finally helps her to confront at least her mother about their shared grief. "'I never saw the baby!' she tells her mother. 'And you never named him!' I began to cry. My voice rose. 'And you never talked to me about him!'" (90). Her voice grows louder as she gains the power that comes from finally articulating the words that have been stifling her. Just as Ms. Minifred and Byrd have asserted, poetry—words—are a source of power for Larkin.

Larkin's father reifies words when he describes them to her: "'Words,' said Papa, softly. 'Did you know that words have a life? They travel out into the air with the speed of sound, a small life of their own, before they disappear. Like the circles that a rock makes when it's tossed into the middle of the pond'" (94). Papa's metaphor adds substance to Larkin's understanding of language: not only does silence have an effect on people; words do, too. When Larkin thinks specifically about the word *love*, she thinks of the word as a being unto itself: "That word with a life of its own, traveling out over the town, over the water, out into the world, flying above all of us like the birds" (97). This metaphor ties together much of the bird imagery that permeates the book and that is most strongly evoked by Byrd's and Lark(in)'s names: we are to understand that words have wings; words are virtually alive.

After Sophie's mother reclaims her, Larkin's family is again immersed in voicelessness to avoid feeling pain. But this time, Byrd forces the issue when she says, "'If we talk about Sophie, we can talk about Larkin's brother who died. The baby she never saw. The baby with no name. . . . Words,' Byrd said" (122). Larkin draws courage from her grandmother's speech and reminds her parents that "even *Sophie* had words" (122). And the family finally begins to talk about the dead baby. The pain begins to heal with the use of words; the reader once again learns that language is a source of agency.

Larkin's parents ultimately allow her to name the dead baby, an action which becomes symbolic of Larkin's vocalization process. Her parents have finally recognized that they have been wrong to silence her, so they compensate by giving her the power of naming someone else. She chooses the name "William," in memory of Ms. Minifred's dead brother who wanted to be a writer and who thought that "words were comforting. Words had power" (84). Silence pervades the ceremony at the graveyard when the family names the baby William; "the only sound was the sound of waves on the outer beach, waves one after the other, like heartbeats" (123). Sound, like language, is a life force that ties people to each other.

After the ceremony, for the first time Larkin is able to follow literally in her father's footsteps; she can finally tap-dance. Her dancing metaphorically represents her recovery of her voice, just as poetry has been Cassie Binegar's venue for recovering hers. But Larkin's dancing is not the joyful exuberance that one might expect from tap, because "for some reason, as I danced I began to cry" (125). She is now making the same noise with her feet that she has admired her father making, but in crying she is also making the noise she has needed to make for herself.

Baby concludes with Larkin's having recovered her voice and having regained the sense of family she has been missing. She has exited from the gap of undecidability that she has been living in because of her parents. Sophie, too, gains a stronger voice, for as a ten year old she puts words to the images from her memory. And language—"the power of wondrous words"—is affirmed as the only force which can both define the individual and bring people together. The affirmation is especially important as it is experienced by two girls, Larkin and Sophie, who were once silent but who are now vocal.

Minfong Ho's *Rice without Rain* (1990) also exemplifies how central a speaking voice is to female development. The story is about Jinda Boonreung's participation in the student demonstration at Thammasart University, Thailand, in 1976. Published on the heels of the massacre at Tiananmen Square in June 1989, *Rice without Rain* makes clear that having a voice within one's culture is both a personal and a political imperative.

Jinda lives with her family in a farming village. Because of a two-year drought, they are slowly starving; Jinda's infant nephew even dies of malnutrition. Recognizing that traditional gender roles are part of what entraps their culture, Jinda admits that "flirting looked like fun, with its soft laughter and quick whispers. But what did it lead to? A howling baby within a year and an unbroken cycle of swollen bellies and milk-heavy breasts after that. Jinda had seen that happen to her sister and countless other village girls, and she vowed that she would not let the same thing happen to her" (15). Among the people of her own village, however, Jinda has always had a secure voice, laughing louder than her sister thinks is appropriate. But since their grandmother also has a raucous laugh, Jinda's laughter is a mark of matrilineal strength.

When a group of revolutionary students arrive in the village asking to work there so that they can learn more about the people of their own land, Jinda begins to lose her voice. She befriends Sri, a medical student, and Ned, the group's leader, but cannot tell them the many things she thinks about them. For example, Jinda is offended when Sri refuses to drink the water from the family well. She tells Jinda, "I will help you boil some drinking water later" (33). "Go boil yourself, Jinda felt like saying. Instead, she stalked into the kitchen and furiously poked the cooking fire" (33). Sri is then so repulsed by the family's dinner that Jinda tells her that it is actually the pigs' dinner. Sri gives Jinda some of the dried fish she has brought with her, but Sri does not know how to prepare it. Jinda slices it "without a word" and then listens patiently while Sri explains: "Ned says Thai students don't use their hands enough. . . . All we have ever been taught to do is think" (36–37). Jinda, still silencing herself, thinks, "Then how come you never thought to look at our pigsty and see that it's empty?" (37). Jinda, nevertheless, is unable to voice her strong opinions because she is too intimidated by these intellectuals.

Sri often quotes Ned's ideas in another type of silencing the book demonstrates: women too often surrender to men's authority, even within intellectual circles. Before Jinda can learn to live the way she wants to live, she must learn to stand up to men like Ned and voice her own opinions. When Ned and Sri leave the village, Jinda stays behind. She tries to correspond with Ned but stops when he corrects the spelling in her letter. She feels effectively silenced by his criticism. She finally travels to Bangkok when Ned sends her a round-trip ticket and asks her to come help their cause. Although she tells Ned that she is aware he thinks of her as a political pawn, more as a symbol of the oppressed Thai farmer than as a person, she decides to stay in Bangkok and join the protest with him when he tells her that he thinks of her romantically. Eventually, however, she recognizes that ideas are more important to Ned than people are, that ideals are more important to him than she is. She says to him, "Can you taste justice? Can you smell equality? What do all your fancy words mean? I can't live my life for things that I can't taste, or smell, or hold in my hands. Soil after the rain, it has such a rich, sweet smell. And tamarind shoots leave a golden taste on your tongue. These things are real. These things I can live for" (217). Finally finding the voice to be completely honest with Ned, Jinda tells him to go fight his revolution without her, for she plans to stay in her farming community fostering life rather than taking it.

Jinda then helps her sister give birth to a baby girl whose birth coincides symbolically with a drought-breaking rain. Jinda's happiness that the baby is a girl communicates that matriarchal values have political import. Jinda's niece arrives with the fertile rain while her nephew died in the drought, symbolizing the text's political values: the violence associated with man-made wars can never end poverty. By Ho's definition, wars are sterile. As the text concludes, Jinda begins to think of her father's death not as a political symbol in the way Ned encouraged her to consider it but as a personal triumph, an act of giving for his children. "Ned was wrong. Her father hadn't died for justice, or equality, or democracy. Like the strong green rice stalks that shrivel as the grain ripens, her father had given up his life for his children, so that they might grow stronger. And he had done it out of love" (234). The conflation of three events coincides with the development of Jinda's voice: Jinda refuses to join Ned's revolutionary group, her niece is born, and Jinda recognizes that her father was motivated more by a personal love for his family than by the abstract ideals of the revolutionaries. Jinda has ascertained what is important to her and has acted upon that decision. Her decision carries overt political overtones that advocate pacifism in a war-torn country.

Rice without Rain has a significant number of implications for feminist readers. On the most basic level, it communicates about the necessity of voice. Building on that concept, the text makes clear that articulation cannot occur until the individual has established her own values. But *Rice without Rain* also privileges a certain set of values that has both personal and political implications: the maintenance of the life cycle is more important than abstract political ideals.

Rice without Rain shares with *Let the Circle Be Unbroken* a concern for the silencing of females of color. Both Jinda and Cassie represent characters who find their voice, but both of them suffer even more social repression than the privileged, middle-class, white protagonists of MacLachlan's novels. Despite the differing degrees of silencing that occur in Taylor's, MacLachlan's, and Ho's narratives, however, all these novels communicate the common ideology that an ability to use her voice is essential to a girl's subjectivity. While the capacity to embrace silence is certainly a necessary component of maturity, the difference between enforced and chosen silence is a monumental one. Self-imposed silence presumes the subject has access to speech. But those who are denied speech, denied language, are also denied their full potential as humans; they are denied community. Language and its articulation provides Cassie Taylor, Cassie Binegar, Larkin, and Jinda Boonreung with the strength they need to participate as full members of their communities so that in the future their silences will be self-affirming, not self-limiting.

5.   RE/CONSTRUCTING THE
        FEMALE WRITER:
        SUBJECTIVITY IN THE
        FEMINIST *KÜNSTLERROMAN*

Margaret Mahy's *The Tricksters* examines what it means to one girl that she is a writer; so does Patricia MacLachlan's *Cassie Binegar*. Both of these novels depict a girl who claims the subject position by learning to use her voice, but significantly, each character learns to use her voice not only as a matter of speaking but also as a matter of writing. Because writing and re-visioning have so much potential to help people understand their agency, quite a few feminist children's novels explore what it means for children to write. The resulting novels seek to explore how children write, why they write, and what they gain as individuals during the process.

One step in understanding such novels is to understand the conventions of the *Bildungsroman*, the novel of development, and of the *Künstlerroman*, the novel of artistic development. In the introduction to *The Voyage In: Fictions of Female Development*, Elizabeth Abel, Marianne Hirsch, and Elizabeth Langland note the traditions of the female *Bildungsroman*. Historically, the female protagonist's growth is less direct than her male counterpart's; the independence that maturation dictates for male characters is often hampered for females by the heroine's belief that she can only develop to her fullest potential if she is intimately involved in relationships with other people. As a result, many female *Bildungsromane* focus on the character's development as a function of the interpersonal relationships she maintains (Abel, Hirsch, and Langland 11). Annis Pratt demonstrates how often the so-called growth of the hero of a female *Bildungsroman* is marked by her retreating from life rather than becoming fully involved in it (36).

As a specialized form of the *Bildungsroman*, the *Künstlerroman* is a novel of development, but the development deals specifically with the growth of the artist. In a number of traditional female *Künstlerromane*, the heroine's self-identification as an artist is either balanced or negated by a love relationship. For example, Jo March gives up her perception of herself as primarily a novelist to marry Professor Bhaer. Judy Abbott "suppose[s] I could keep on being a writer even if I did marry" near the end of *Daddy-Long-Legs*, but since she never mentions writing as a career again, her supposition is unconvincing (181–82). In Betty Smith's *A Tree Grows in Brooklyn* (1943), Francie Nolan makes a pact with God that she will not write anymore if her mother will survive a serious illness. Francie later realizes that she need not necessarily sacrifice her writing forever, but she clearly does not perceive herself primarily as a writer by the novel's end. She concentrates more on going to college and getting married than on writing.

But within the genre of the children's *Künstlerroman* exists a subgenre, the feminist *Künstlerroman*, which demonstrates the growth of a child whose identity is consistently formed by her desire to be a writer. Different from books like Lois Lowry's *Anastasia Krupnik* (1979), wherein writing is only one of the protagonist's myriad activities, the protagonist of the feminist children's *Künstlerroman* is a writer whose writing is her entire being. Furthermore, she never sacrifices her writing for the sake of a love relationship. In "Portrait of the Young Writer in Children's Fiction" (1977), Francis Molson briefly surveys a collection of children's novels about developing writers, including Louise Fitzhugh's *Harriet the Spy* (1964), Irene Hunt's *Up a Road Slowly* (1968), Jean Little's *Look through My Window*, Eleanor Cameron's *A Room Made of Windows* (1971), and Mollie Hunter's *A Sound of Chariots* (1972). Never once does Molson make note of the fact that the young writers of his survey are all female. That so many children's novels involve girls learning about the power of language indicates, however, that the genre is a powerful forum for feminist writers.

Harriet the Spy and *A Sound of Chariots* both exemplify the characteristics of the feminist *Künstlerroman*. The protagonists of these novels accept language as primary to their self-creation, and they live through words, ultimately recognizing that they are powerless without them. In this regard, both of these novels are a study in the use of textual subjectivity, for as each of these girls recognizes the primacy of language in her life, she achieves an understanding of the matrices of subject positions she occupies as a writer, a female, a family member, and a friend. Most important, each of these girls learns to "write her self," to "put herself into the text—as into the world and into history—by her own movement" (Cixous, "Laugh of the Medusa" 875). Each of these feminist writers changes her perception of herself and her world by writing.

Louise Fitzhugh's *Harriet the Spy* is the prototypical feminist children's *Künstlerroman* largely because Harriet is one of the earliest characters to experience a number of the genre's conventions. First, Harriet defines herself as different from other people. She clings to her individualism by wearing androgynous clothing, by eating tomato sandwiches, and by rejecting such signs of social conformity as dance class and bridge club. She also separates herself from other people by spying on them, that is, by putting herself in the subject position and them in the object position. Something of a Peeping Tom, Harriet watches people through windows and cracked doors and then writes down what she has observed because, as she tells a friend, "I've *seen* them and I want to *remember* them" (11). Harriet recognizes that words make her memories permanent. Language thus has great power for her because it is only through words that she can perceive her own past.

Harriet does not necessarily intend to objectify people when she is trying to affix them in her memory, but she nevertheless does. She dons her father's eyeglasses, which could be interpreted as the symbolic spectacles of the patriarchy, before she goes to spy on people, and she sits in judgment of them as she peers through the lenses. She calls Mrs. Plumber "BORING" (45) and Franca Dei Santi "DULL" (57). Of the Robinsons she writes: "SOME PEOPLE THINK THEY'RE PERFECT BUT . . . I'M GLAD I'M NOT PERFECT—I'D BE BORED TO DEATH. BESIDES IF

THEY'RE SO GREAT WHY DO THEY JUST SIT THERE ALL DAY STARING AT NOTHING? THEY COULD BE CRAZY AND NOT EVEN KNOW IT" (68). Harriet has little empathy for these people because she sees them as little more than fodder (objects) with which she can feed her own thoughts and writings.

Harriet, however, defines writing as absolutely crucial to her self-expression. When the notebook in which she records all her thoughts is taken from her, she feels completely powerless: "Without a notebook she couldn't spy, she couldn't take notes, she couldn't play Town, she couldn't do anything. She was afraid to go and buy another one, and for once she didn't feel like reading" (257). As Francis Molson notes, Harriet feels that "words can give external shape" to her imaginative processes ("Another Look" 964), so without her notebooks she feels alienated from her own creativity. Molson adds, "Surely one of the book's strengths is its depiction of Harriet's awareness that she can fully know only when she can verbalize her thoughts" ("Another Look" 965). As is common for the protagonist of the feminist children's *Künstlerroman*, Harriet fully understands how powerful language is only when she analyzes her own need to write.

Another convention of the feminist *Künstlerroman* that Harriet experiences is a disruption of her home life that causes her great grief. Harriet mourns deeply when her nanny, Ole Golly, leaves to get married. In Harriet's case, the grief she feels coincides with ostracism from her community; such ostracism is also a convention of the feminist children's *Künstlerroman*. For Harriet, the rejection of her community occurs shortly after Ole Golly's departure when Harriet's classmates read her private notebooks and begin to shun her. As a result of feeling so isolated from other people, Harriet exhibits yet another convention of the feminist child writer: she learns to shift her subject position.

That Harriet needs to learn to shift her subjectivity is clearly outlined in the novel. For example, early in the narrative Harriet wonders how lonely she would be flying around space if the universe blows up. Harriet does not perceive that she, too, would be destroyed along with everyone else (79). Later, Harriet egocentrically assumes that Mr. Waldenstein will move in with Ole Golly in the bedroom next to Harriet's after they get married (97). Ironically, Harriet accuses her mother of not thinking "about other people much" (102). Harriet certainly thinks of other people, but only as the objects of her spying; at this point in the novel she is incapable of even temporarily imagining their subject positions.

But eventually Harriet develops the ability to see herself as other people might. As part of the persecution she receives at the hands of her classmates, someone spills ink all over Harriet. The scene takes on the significance of being a ritual baptism, for after Harriet is washed in the metaphorical waters of her chosen profession, she has the epiphany that enables her to switch subject positions. Significantly, she actually employs linguistics to define this switch. When she realizes that her classmates have named the secret club they have formed THE SPY CATCHER CLUB, she thinks, "So it was she, Harriet, that they were talking about. She was *her*. How odd, she thought, to think of yourself as *her*" (223). Harriet initially identifies herself with grammatical correctness by using the nominative pronoun that the verb "to be" requires. But then she ungrammatically shifts her self-identification to the objective pronoun: "She was *her*." Far from being a simple lapse of grammar, the change in pronoun case signifies the first time that Harriet is capable of perceiving herself as other people do and as she has perceived other people: in the object position.

Shortly after this experience, the text articulates an aesthetic philosophy which can guide Harriet. This articulation, itself a convention of the feminist children's *Künstlerroman*, triggers another convention of novels about feminist child writers when Harriet transforms her private writing into public writing. As with many feminist *Künstlerromane*, the aesthetic philosophy is inspired by a mentor.[1] Ole Golly writes to Harriet and tells her, "*If you are ever going to be a writer it is time you got cracking. You are eleven years old and haven't written a thing but notes*" (275). Ole Golly quotes John Keats on truth and beauty to remind Harriet that as an art form, writing is a way to create beauty and express truths.[2] Then, in a classic moment of self-contradiction, Ole Golly tells Harriet that sometimes she is going to have to lie about her writing. Ole Golly justifies her advice: "*Remember that writing is to put love in the world, not to use against your friends. But to yourself you must always tell the truth*" (276). The greatest weakness in *Harriet the Spy* is in this statement of the text's aesthetic philosophy. Ole Golly's advice is little more than the classic feminine reversion to deceit to survive in the patriarchal world. Nevertheless, the advice—traditional as it is—gives Harriet the ability to share her writing with other people. She writes a story that she sends to the *New Yorker*, and then she begins to write for her school newspaper.

This act marks the final and most crucial stage of the feminist children's *Künstlerroman*. In traditional male *Künstlerromane* such as *Portrait of the Artist as a Young Man*, the writer rejects his community and decides to pursue his art isolated from the sullying influence of a philistine world. In the traditional female *Künstlerroman*, however, the female writer often gives up her primary identity as a writer: to wit, Jo March perceives her roles as wife, mother, and headmistress as more important than her role as a writer by the end of *Little Women*. Thus, as Marianne Hirsch notes, male heroes in nineteenth-century *Künstlerromane* find a salvation in art that helps them avoid the female's almost mandated death, for pursuing art is rarely a resolution that female characters could pursue during that era ("Spiritual *Bildung*" 28). For male protagonists, the *Künstlerroman* establishes imagination and the inward life as a "solution" to the struggles he experiences, but for nineteenth-century female protagonists, focusing inward results only in stultification (Hirsch, "Spiritual *Bildung*" 46–47).

Like Harriet the Spy, Jo March has perceived herself as outside her culture. She has experienced the domestic grief of Beth's death, she has gone public with her writing, and she has learned to shift her subject position when she (unfortunately) perceives herself through Professor Bhaer's eyes. She even views herself through his "moral spectacles" in much the same way that Harriet wears her father's glasses: "Being a little shortsighted, Mr. Bhaer sometimes used eyeglasses, and Jo had tried them once, smiling to see how they magnified the fine print of her book; now she seemed to have got on the Professor's mental or moral spectacles also, for the faults of these poor stories glared at her dreadfully and filled her with dismay" (*Little Women* 322). Nevertheless, despite undergoing many of the stages of the feminist *Künstlerroman* that Harriet experiences, eventually Jo ceases to identify herself primarily as a writer.[3] As Hirsch notes of many nineteenth-century novels by women, art is ultimately not a solution for Jo as a female protagonist ("Spiritual *Bildung*" 28).

Investigating the nuances of the *Künstlerroman* within children's literature, Jan Alberghene observes that in American children's books, artists often learn to place their community before their art. Many child characters in such novels decide that their community is more important than their individual need for artistic expression (*From Alcott* 1). But the feminist children's *Künstlerroman* modifies the paradigmatic endings of the (adult) male, the (adult) female, and the children's *Künstlerroman*. As in the typical children's *Künstlerroman*, the feminist protagonist reconciles herself to her community, but with this significant difference: she insists on maintaining her primary identity as a writer, as the protagonist of a traditional male *Künstlerroman* does and as the protagonist of a traditional female *Künstlerroman* does not.

Thus, at the end of *Harriet the Spy*, Harriet reconciles herself to her friends and identifies with them in a traditionally female act of empathy. In the final pages, she sees her closest friends, Janie and Sport, approaching her in the park, and she thinks:

> They were so far away that they looked like dolls. They made her think of the way she imagined the people when she played Town. Somehow this way she could see them better than she ever had before. She looked at them each carefully in the longish time it took them to reach her. She made herself walk in Sport's shoes, feeling the holes in his socks rub against his ankles. She pretended she had an itchy nose when Janie put one abstracted hand up to scratch. She felt what it would feel like to have freckles and yellow hair like Janie, then funny ears and skinny shoulders like Sport. (297)

Harriet has certainly learned to shift her subject position and to do what it takes to reconcile herself with her culture. But more important, she still identifies herself as a writer. One of the final sentences in the book is something Harriet writes in her journal: "NOW THAT THINGS ARE BACK TO NORMAL I CAN GET SOME REAL WORK DONE" (298). The final sentences, "She slammed the book and stood up. All three of them turned then and walked along the river" (298), show that Harriet has learned to work within her community without sacrificing her art.

Lissa Paul calls *Harriet the Spy* "a successful female *künstlerroman*" because a "double feminist trick is in play": Harriet "tricks" her classmates into accepting her journals as fiction when she writes them up for the school paper, and Fitzhugh "tricks critics" into approving of the text's duplicitous morality ("Feminist Writer" 67). Paul defines the following as feminist conventions at work in *Harriet the Spy*: Harriet "prefers a small-scale form of writing (the private notebook); she juggles her role in society (her popularity with her classmates) with her role as a writer (which demands selfishness); she is concerned with being truthful, but ultimately discovers that that necessitates lying; and she finds that domestic gossip constitutes a valid form of fiction" (67). I would argue that the "small-scale form" of Harriet's writing has as much to do with her being a child as her being female and that the juggling act between the writer's social and artistic roles is a concern in most *Künstlerromane*, regardless of the protagonist's gender. And while Paul's assessment of Harriet's deceit as a female survival tactic is accurate, I hesitate to label this duplicity "feminist." I think, instead, Harriet is accepting a traditional gender role. What seems to me to be more feminist about the text is Harriet's refusal to give up her identity as writer. No matter how much pressure her parents, teachers, and friends exert on her, as the novel ends she is still triumphantly a writer.

Mollie Hunter's *A Sound of Chariots*, a largely autobiographical *Künstlerroman*, also demonstrates many of the conventions of the feminist children's *Künstlerroman*, despite a historical setting that might initially seem to preclude an articulation of feminist values.[4] Bridie McShane is a young girl in post–World War I Scotland who uses writing to come to terms with her father's death. Unlike *Harriet the Spy*, which gradually builds toward the disequilibrium of grief that Ole Golly's departure causes Harriet, *A Sound of Chariots* opens with the death that causes the protagonist's acute sense of alienation. Thus, the entire novel is about Bridie's attempts to reconcile herself to her community while she develops artistically. Writing proves to be the means through which she effects this reconciliation.

Bridie perceives herself as a writer before her father ever dies; in fact, it is he who suggests that she might one day write a book (61). Because of his belief in her, she proudly proclaims, "I'm going to be an *authoress*!" (81). Her proclamation leads her sisters to mock her:

"Author-*ass*! Author-*ass*!" (81). Her love of language makes her different from her sisters, and this difference is the source of their ostracism. Not only does she feel no sense of community with them, but she also even labels them "the Others" to confirm her own subject position by objectifying them.

Despite her sisters' teasing, Bridie loves words, "for the sound and the feel of them and the marvelous way they allowed her to unlock ideas from her mind" (82). Her metaphor for the writing experience is to describe herself as being like a prompter at a play: "The difference was that the copy she had was being written out while the play went on, and it was not she who prompted the actors. When she was stuck for a word, they prompted her" (84). Her understanding of language is both passive and postmodern: language exists as an exterior force that constructs who she is and what she writes. Yet Bridie's father has told her that "everyone's entitled to a private place in the mind" (111). She may be constructed by language, but she is, nevertheless and indisputably, an individual.

Although Bridie has established an identity for herself as a writer before her father's death, she does not fully understand the power that language can give her until she seeks a means to reconcile the subject/object split that she experiences as a result of her grief for her father. Bridie has been her father's favorite child, so his death devastates the nine-year-old girl. Although she has valued her mother's affection, it is her father's approbation that means the most to her. In the final outing before his death, while gazing at a photograph of herself, Bridie sees how much she physically resembles her father. The resulting feeling of connection she feels with him gives her great pleasure (114). But after he dies, she feels even more isolated from her community than she has before: "Everything seemed slower and quieter than it had been before and nothing that happened seemed to connect directly with her" (119).

Moreover, she experiences an increasing sense of terror as she recognizes her own mortality. She has a recurring nightmare in which she experiences herself as a fragmented body:

> The nightmare . . . always took the same form. All the men in
> their street—the blind men, the legless, the armless ones—were
> standing in a silent, motionless group outside the wooden fence

surrounding the little graveyard in front of the church. They were all looking in the same direction. . . . The something they were gazing at was a dismembered body. She could see all the different parts of it, each lying in the pool of its own blood, and as she watched she saw that each of the dismembered limbs was moving as if it was still alive. Then she became aware that the sound she could hear was the head crying feebly aloud, and with a rush of pity she realized that the body *was* alive and that its separated head was crying desperately for help.

None of the cripples moved to help it. She cried urgently to them, *"It's still alive! Help it, please help it!"* But the group of misshapen men, as if they had not heard her, continued to stand there as silent and motionless as some grotesque waxworks show.

She had to help it. It was impossible to leave the poor thing there, crying out like that. She crept towards it. The head turned and looked at her. She saw her own face and realized that the thing was herself. (122)

A powerful evocation of the fragmented self, this passage's depiction of corporeal dismemberment is not unlike some of the imagery Margaret Atwood employs in *The Edible Woman* (1969) and *Surfacing* (1972) to represent women's fragmentation in modern culture. Although initially in the dream Bridie feels that she has some agency, for it is she who must help the fragmented body, when Bridie sees herself not only in the object position of the veterans' gazes but as an actual object, a "thing," she loses that sense of her own agency and becomes immobilized.

This sense of powerlessness comes from her fear of death, her recognition that if death "could happen to [her father], *it could happen to her!"* (133). The passage that leads to this recognition emphasizes the importance of Bridie's subject position. As she and her brother and sisters prepare to bury a rabbit that has died, "She *saw* that Moira and Aileen and William looked very solemn and that Nell had an earnest, uplifted expression on her face. But close as they all were to her, she had the curious impression that they were tiny and faraway *as if she was seeing them through the wrong end of the telescope"* (131, emphasis added). Bridie runs away from "the Others" because she fears she is going blind, and she ends up standing in the lane, where she recognizes her own mortality. But her anagnorisis, that is, her moment of self-recognition, has been clearly predicated on shifting her subject position; her blindness is replaced by a confusing vision of herself as both subject and object.

Bridie experiences this anagnorisis in terms as visceral as her nightmares have been. "In panic revulsion from the thought she jerked upright as if she could pull herself physically away from it," but she scrapes her hand across some brier-rose thorns (133). As she watches the blood that oozes from the scratches, she thinks: "This *was* her life, these shiny red drops welling from her skin, and with the inescapable fact that she would die some day still beating in her brain she was suddenly seeing them with an acuteness of vision that made it seem as if a skin had been peeled from her eyes" (133). Bridie is experiencing a subject split: is she object/blood or is she subject/vision?

This split is exacerbated when Bridie goes to pick violets for her mother's birthday. Bridie has been overwhelmed by her mother's grief and hopes that the flowers will comfort the grieving woman. The girl climbs over a stone fence to get to the bank where the flowers grow and lands in a pile of lambs' tails that a shepherd has recently shorn. Bridie is repulsed at the "blood and bits of bodies" (156); this dismemberment scene seems to be an enactment of her nightmare. But Bridie grows because of this virtual immersion in corporality. She has literally bathed herself in the blood of the lamb; the paschal image is reinforced when she shares red wine and bread with the shepherd's wife, who tries to calm the hysterical girl. And after sharing this female communion, Bridie can finally separate herself from her mother's grief:

> She didn't care about her mother now because she just couldn't bear any more horrifying things to happen. She was finished with her mother's grief now, finished with it. She wouldn't think about it ever again. She couldn't bear to think of it or the thing she had dreaded would come true again. The nightmare of the body in the churchyard would come smothering down on her in broad daylight like it had when her face had been pressed down into the blood and bits of bodies and she would scream and scream and scream till her head exploded in screaming. (158)

The blood imagery prefigures Bridie's menarche, which is a vital stage in her maturation (228–29), but Bridie's recognition of herself as separate from her mother is an even more crucial stage in her artistic development. She is beginning to recognize that her interior world is the source of her own agency.

Bridie's employer, Mr. Purves, cautions Bridie: "You think too much and you see too much and it's all there in your face" (180). This "revelation" causes Bridie to lead what she considers a double life; she learns to act like "an empty-headed chatterbox" to conceal that "underneath this there was the other part of her mind, like another person watching all her antics and observing the effect they had" (182–83). Bridie is still living in the subject/object split, viewing herself dispassionately but still significantly engaged in the act of viewing. She intentionally uses the double position that this split affords her as a way to separate herself from her fear of "*Time's wingèd chariot hurrying near*" (194). When she engages her subjectivity to view herself in the object position, she feels victorious: "As if she was on a different plane then, another level of living entirely from the moment as it existed for those taking part in it, she would see it suddenly projected with a strange, objective clarity in front of her. And with a thrill of triumph she would know that she had snatched yet another moment from the wasteful stream of living running past her; another moment of time had been caught and petrified forever in her memory" (215). Like Harriet, Bridie considers memory a form of self-definition, and like Harriet, she recognizes that memory is language-bound.

Bridie's capacity to understand herself with a double vision ultimately becomes the aesthetic philosophy that underpins *A Sound of Chariots*. The text insists that a writer must be someone who both lives in the world and who removes herself from it to view it objectively. This doubleness turns the novel into a triumphant admixture of the traditional male *Künstlerroman* and the feminist children's *Künstlerroman*: the writer should be simultaneously detached from and immersed in her community.

Grace Stewart notes that this sense of double vision is a convention in the *Künstlerroman*, but she argues, "Whereas the man feels split between personal and social being, the woman experiences that split and the separation of sexual and personal identity" (175). Bridie does seem to have difficulty with her sexual identity. Her fondest early memories include being her father's favorite child because she is a tomboy, and later she rejects menstruation, declaring, "I won't have it! I won't *let* it happen to me!" (227). Stewart notes that in many *Künstlerromane* written by women, birds are mutilated in some way or another (177). As an image of artistic freedom, birds show the destruction of the female artist. Yet in *A Sound of Chariots* it is not birds who are shown to be destroyed; instead, it is a rabbit, a traditional symbol of female fertility, that is dead. When linked with Bridie's androgyny, the dead rabbit indicates the girl's rejection of one traditional role of the female subject: that of procreator.

Like Harriet, Bridie has a mentor, her English teacher, Dr. McIntyre, who directly advises her about what it means to be a writer. He calls Bridie "a poet-in-embryo" and chants her name over and over (219) in a passage that Sarah Smedman identifies as "a kind of ritualistic calling her forth to and priestly confirmation of her sacred vocation" (137). Dr. McIntyre also reinforces the double aesthetics of *A Sound of Chariots* when he tells Bridie that experience "can only be constructive if the subject of it succeeds in building *outwards* from it. Otherwise, there is only a self-destructive burrowing-inwards, a futile self-consumption of intellect that is the antithesis of creativeness. For creativeness, my child, is all outgoing. It is experience absorbed and put forth again in a finer form" (220). Here McIntyre seems to be counseling Bridie to write for other people, as Ole Golly might say, "*To put love in the world*" (Fitzhugh 276). But later, McIntyre reminds Bridie that "you always will be alone. . . . Alone in your mind, that is, for you have chosen the loneliest of all vocations—or rather, I should say, it has chosen you" (237). This time, McIntyre articulates the masculine mythos of the poet as removed from any community. Note, however, that McIntyre's metaphor places Bridie in the object position: poetry has chosen her rather than her choosing to be a poet. The metaphor implies the primacy of language: language constructs the subject rather than the subject constructing language.

McIntyre's most compelling advice to Bridie is for her to "*live*" for her father: "Don't let your talent die because he is dead. Let it flower from his death and speak for both of you!" (238). McIntyre's advice is not the paternal advice that it initially might seem to be; it is not an insistence that Bridie become her father, for she interprets it to mean that she should use her memory of her father and the pain she has felt as the inspiration to become the writer she wants to be. Although grief has caused her to feel alienated from other people, it has also provided her with the inspiration to write, and through writing, she finally feels reconnected to the world. For example, by the end of the novel, Bridie has learned to work with her sisters at communal tasks (165), and she has openly acknowledged her acceptance of her mother and the pride she feels for her (213, 239). These reconciliations mark Bridie's readiness to move to a larger community where she can work and send her wages home to help support her family. Thus, ironically, Bridie takes her place in the community by leaving it.

In the novel's final image, Bridie rides a tram to her new home in Edinburgh. She describes seeing "a great vase of full-blown roses, white roses looking with soft, ghostly faces at her out of the purple-black darkness of the empty room behind them" (242). She has left the familiar community of her childhood home, so in a sense she is like the roses, which have reached maturity but bloom removed from their community. She feels herself to be a "galleon plunging through perilous seas," but her guiding star will be the poetry she will write. And she has maintained her self-image of herself as a writer. The final lines in the text assert that all she will need to write is "a little light, a little time" (242); all she will need is a room of her own. The ramifications for feminism are important. Bridie clearly feels herself at one with language. So, for that matter, does Harriet. In fact, the only way these girls know how to define themselves is through language. Through language and in writing, they accept their own subjectivities, gaining a voice and rejecting the silencing that their cultures seem to expect of them.

The protagonist of the feminist children's *Künstlerroman* need not necessarily be female. For example, Beverly Cleary's *Dear Mr. Henshaw* displays a number of the genre's conventions, even though the androgynously named protagonist, Leigh Botts, is male. He suffers from the grief caused by his parents' divorce; he feels like an outsider because his mother and he moved after the divorce; he feels ostracized because someone steals the best part of his lunch every day. He has a mentor, the children's author, Mr. Henshaw, who inspires him to write, although it is actually Leigh's mother who articulates the text's aesthetic philosophy after she reads a letter from Mr. Henshaw. Leigh writes to tell Mr. Henshaw his mother's advice: "She says . . . I should read, look, listen, think and *write*" (14). Leigh goes public with his writing when his school sponsors a writing contest. He has a moment of self-recognition when his writing is validated by a woman who is a published author. She calls him an "author," and she tells him he writes well because "you wrote like *you*, and you did not try to imitate someone else" (118, 119–20). By the end of the novel, Leigh has accepted himself as a writer and has been accepted into his community. If his self-acceptance seems more inevitable than Harriet's or Bridie's has, perhaps that is because he is a male in a culture where assuming the role of writer has been more easily granted to men than women, but the novel is still more feminist than not in its workings.[5]

Not every novel written in the last thirty years about a child writer qualifies as a feminist children's *Künstlerroman*, however. Sheila Greenwald has written a number of novels that involve girls who are developing their talents at writing, most notably *It All Began with Jane Eyre: Or, the Secret Life of Franny Dillman* (1980) and the books in her *Rosy Cole* series. Greenwald's books are humorous and her protagonists are spunky, but they use their writing talents primarily as a way to get involved in romantic relationships. Franny Dillman's greatest achievement does not seem to be the book she's written; it's that she's finally been noticed by a boy. Ditto for Rosy Cole in *Rosy's Romance* (1989).

Even books as disparate as Ellen Conford's *Jenny Archer, Author* (1989) and Barbara Wersba's *Love Is the Crooked Thing* (1987) are not this obvious. Although written for quite a young reading audience, *Jenny Archer* learns the difference between creating fiction and nonfiction, and she finds her imaginative creativity affirmed. Similarly, although the protagonist of the young adult novel *Love Is the Crooked Thing* initially worries more about her relationship with her boyfriend than anything, eventually she realizes that her writing matters more to her than he does. While neither Conford's nor Wersba's book develops a protagonist who learns to "write herself," as Cixous would say, their books display more of the conventions of the feminist children's *Künstlerroman* than Greenwald's books do.

While Michael Cadden was a graduate student in one of my seminars, he pointed out that the biggest difference between traditional and feminist children's *Künstlerromane* is that in the feminist ones, the texts end before the child protagonist grows up and "gets boring," as he put it; that is, the novel ends before the protagonist enters the typical gender-encoded roles of courtship. Annis Pratt refers to this pattern as "dwarfing" or "dulling a hero's initiative and restraining her maturation" (41). Jo March in *Little Women*, Judy Abbott in *Daddy-Long-Legs*, Francie Nolan in *A Tree Grows in Brooklyn*, Julie Bishop in *Up a Road Slowly*, and Julia Redfern in *The Private Worlds of Julia Redfern* (1988) all end up as young adults preoccupied by love interests; they lose the sense of autonomy that has made them interesting characters in the first place.

That Eleanor Cameron's *Julia Redfern* series ends with Julia's immersion in a romantic relationship seems particularly disappointing. After all, she is a girl who, like Bridie McShane, recognizes the interiority of the writing process:

> As I'm writing, I'm hearing and seeing it all—the story—and it's like a play, because there's the dialogue and you're listening inside your head to just how a person would say something. You have to hear the tone and the way of saying and the rhythm, just as you do onstage when you're rehearsing your lines. And you're *seeing* it all happen. If you can't, how could you know what each character is doing every moment, in relation to the others, just how they're sitting or standing or turning and moving off the stage of your scene. (*The Private Worlds* 194)

The process makes Julia feel powerful: she is the creator of whole worlds. And like Harriet, Julia recognizes herself as a writer when she is quite young (*That Julia Redfern* 15–17); she even publishes at an early age (*A Room Made of Windows* 267). But in having the luxury of developing a character over the course of five novels, Cameron transforms Julia from a rebellious child artist into a fairly predictable lovelorn adolescent. Although Julia does not give up her identity as a writer (which is what keeps the series from being nonfeminist), by the end of the final volume of the series, when Julia feels "unaccountably joyous and hopeful" (218), her hopes are directed not toward her writing ambitions but toward her boyfriend's return (which is what keeps the series from being strongly feminist, either).

Feminist children's *Künstlerromane* demonstrate protagonists who recognize their agency because of their writing. Novels in the genre share a number of characteristics, but the most important is the character's immersion in language that allows her to emerge as an artist who participates in her community without sacrificing her art. Her art and her voice are one. The protagonist of the feminist children's *Künstlerroman* transcends the obstacles that confront her and emerges a fledgling artist.

6. FEMALE INTERDEPENDENCY:

LITERAL AND METAPHORIC

SISTERHOOD

T he protagonists of *Harriet the Spy* and *The Sound of Chariots* explore the nature of their subjectivity through the process of writing; for them, writing is an extension of voice. Voice is an equally important issue in many feminist novels that focus on the importance of human interdependency. A chief characteristic of feminist children's novels is that they define relationships that foster community as an arena in which children of both sexes can safely articulate their voices.

One of the strengths traditionally associated with femininity is the way many women have recognized the importance of community. Throughout history, women have been depicted in their families and friendships as nurturers. This is not to say that all women are nurturers or that men cannot or do not build community as effectively as women do, for they most certainly are capable of the same levels of relationship building. The ability to maintain interrelationships is not genetically linked to sex. But feminist novelists often use the common conception of women strengthening each other within relationships as a focal point. In other words, feminist novelists often embrace the positive aspects of stereotypes about females and use them to their advantage.

It is important to note, however, that community can only occur among people who respect each other's subjectivity. Women and girls need to recognize and engage their agency in order to form healthy interrelationships.[1] This sense of community is a central principle of Carol Gilligan's *In a Different Voice: Psychological Theory and Women's Development* (1982). Drawing on Nancy Chodorow's work on the reproduction of mothering, Gilligan discusses the cultural forces in our society that all too often lead males to feel threatened by emotional intimacy while women feel threatened by emotional separation (8). Gilligan asserts that because of being socialized this way, males and females often have differing images of relationships. The oft-quoted metaphors that Gilligan uses to typify the differences between the genders are of a ladder, evoking how male thinking often focuses on hierarchies, and of a cobweb, evoking how female thinking often focuses on networks (24–63).

In a 1993 article in the *Atlantic*, Wendy Kaminer offers the standard feminist critique of Gilligan as a tendency to essentialize (59). "Essentializing" is the practice of linking specific character traits to sex as if they are biologically determined. For example, some people believe that it is part of the essence of women's souls to nurture or that the essence of masculinity necessitates aggression. Kaminer also cites the feminist tendency to use Gilligan's principles to attribute positive traits to women and negative ones to men (62). I hope, however, to avoid such simplistic binaries. Nowhere do I mean to imply that men are biologically incapable of sustaining close, nurturing relationships or that male authors are incapable of portraying such relationships in their literature, because I believe gender roles are not innate or biologically determined. Instead, I hold the belief that people are constructed into their gender roles by what they learn about "performing" their gender from societal influences (Butler 139).

But Diana Fuss complicates the debate between essentialists like Gilligan and constructivists like me when she demonstrates how often constructivists still rely on concepts that "always already" exist like "male" and "female" to make their arguments (18–21). Fuss encourages feminists to think about the interrelationships between essentialist rhetoric and constructivist rhetoric as a way to broaden our understanding of gender. The debate is a crucial one for all feminist scholars, for if we believe people learn their gender roles, we have a very different perspective than if we believe their anatomy determines their behavior. As Kathleen Chamberlain once noted to me, people's "femaleness" or "maleness" most likely results from both biological *and* social forces.

My hope for feminist children's literature is that it can encourage readers of both sexes to question their own assumptions about gender and that ultimately such texts can demonstrate interrelationships sustaining all people. As Trinh T. Minh-ha argues, "difference" need not necessarily dictate "otherness" (152). People can value the desire to connect that is often associated with traditional femininity without fearing that to focus on interrelationships will make them somehow suspect, somehow Other.

I have noticed, however, that feminist children's novelists frequently rely on character traits often ascribed essentially to females as the foundation for creating strong characters. Rather than depicting female characters who eschew any characteristic typically associated with women, feminist novels often claim as a positive force those characteristics that have sometimes been used to denigrate women. Thus, female characters in this genre often are nurturing, communicative, and sensitive. But equally important is the fact that many of these authors' male characters display the same characteristics. For example, Carol Matas's *The Burning Time* comes the closest to male bashing of any recently published adolescent novel that I have read, but two male characters within this book are still sensitive, communicative, and supportive of their wives and mothers. And several of the female characters are insensitive, treacherous, and just plain mean.

Children's literature has often focused quite naturally on interrelationships, perhaps because of social imperatives that dictate that children should be socialized through their books, or perhaps as a result of being such a female-dominated field. In "Feminist Criticism and the Study of Children's Literature," Anita Moss discusses how the writers, teachers, and authors of children's literature have historically been predominately female (3); Perry Nodelman expounds on that observation in "Children's Literature as Women's Writing" (32). Family interrelationships have thus been central to myriad children's novels, including those by Louisa May Alcott, Noel Streatfield, L. M. Montgomery, Margaret Sidney, and Eleanor Estes. The focus of these interrelationships, however, has often been the reproduction of mothering; the familial relationships in these books are portrayed as a way for girls to train to be mothers or to take on traditional roles within the family structure as a social institution. Chodorow calls the reproduction of mothering

> a central and constituting element in the social organization and reproduction of gender. . . . It is neither a product of biology nor of intentional role-training. . . . Women, as mothers, produce daughters with mothering capacities and the desire to mother. These capacities and needs are built into and grow out of the mother-daughter relationship itself. By contrast, women as mothers (and men as not-mothers) produce sons whose nurturant capacities and needs have been systematically curtailed and repressed. . . . The sexual and familial division of labor in which women mother and are more involved in interpersonal, affective relationships than men produces in daughters and sons a division of psychological capacities which leads them to reproduce this sexual and familial division of labor. (7)

Alcott's March family trilogy and the *Anne of Green Gables* series demonstrate this pattern: childhood relationships and games pave the way for the maternal roles that Jo and Anne adopt as adults.

One revisionary way that some feminists have incorporated the strengths of traditional femininity into their politics is by continuing to embrace the importance of interpersonal relationships, so that feminist children's novels often focus on networks of relationships and how human interdependency can succor the child, but without necessarily requiring her to grow up and be a mother. The key here is "interdependency," which is significantly different from "dependency." Dependency implies a hierarchical model with one person more dependent on (and therefore less powerful than) another; interdependency involves a mutual dependency that emphasizes equality. The purpose of this interdependency in a feminist novel focuses more on the child's or adolescent's development as an individual than on

her being inculcated into a prescribed social role. Rather than relying on her family or community to teach her how to continue in the
repressed roles that women have so long been forced into, the protagonist of a feminist children's novel will learn from relationships
how to take the subject position as a strong and independent person.
Some feminist children's and adolescent novels focus on community
as a general concept important to children of both genders; others focus on strong females within heterosexual relationships; and still others work actively to advocate the strengthening of female bonds between friends, between sisters, and between mothers and daughters.
But whichever of these foci a feminist text takes, its child or adolescent protagonist is likely to assume a subject position that allows her
or him to value community without sacrificing his or her selfhood.

COMMUNITY

Cynthia Rylant is clearly concerned with human interrelationships.
A Blue-Eyed Daisy (1985), *A Fine White Dust* (1986), and *A Kindness*
(1988) all investigate various aspects of the need for human interdependency. More than any of Rylant's other novels, however, *Missing
May* (1992) poignantly depicts the importance of community in a
child's growth. The first-person narrator, Summer, tells the story of
how she and Ob, her foster father, come to reconcile themselves to
the grief they have felt since her foster mother's death. Early in the
book, Summer imagines what May would tell her about their sorrow: "She'd tell us to hold on tight because we're all meant to be together. We're all meant to need each other" (23). When Summer
senses that Ob is beginning to give up because of the depth of his
grief, she decides to do just that, to "hold on tight" to Ob. With a boy
from her seventh-grade class named Cletus, Summer and Ob travel
to the state capital in search of a woman, the Reverend Miriam
Young, who reputedly knows how to speak to the dead. But when
she, too, turns out to have died, Ob seems to despair. Ob manages,
however, to overcome his despondency, perhaps because he recognizes his responsibility to his foster daughter, perhaps because he
feels her holding on tight to him. The novel is about Ob's growth as
much as it is about Summer's, so one of the two protagonists of this
novel is a nurturing, sensitive man.

In the novel's climax, an owl flying through their home reminds Summer of May. Sighting the owl helps Summer cry about her grief; she has been unable to do so until she is sure that Ob will not give up on her. In the penultimate passage, which is narrated by May, the woman reminds Summer of the time they saw an owl together after Summer first came to live with May and Ob. *"I'd not ever seen an owl in all my days, and when I hadn't had you but a few weeks there that one passed through my life. I knew you'd always be doing that for me and for Ob. Bringing us good things like that"* (86). May concludes her monologue by saying, *"We wanted a family so bad, all of us. And we just grabbed onto each another and made us one. Simple as that"* (87).

Whether these words have come from a memory, a dream, or a ghost is unclear, but after hearing them, Ob is able to move his works of art, his whirligigs, outdoors for the first time where they are metaphorically free to fly in the wind. Because Ob and Summer have continued to hold on to each other, they, too, will be able to fly. No longer fettered by their sorrow, they are able to live with some measure of happiness. And they are both stronger people for understanding and accepting death and the mutability of life within a communal environment.

Although Virginia Hamilton emphasizes racial issues even more than gender issues, she is nevertheless an author whose advocacy of interpersonal relationships as a way to strengthen community is often feminist in nature. For instance, *M. C. Higgins the Great* (1974) is a story that combines an African American sense of community with a feminist sense of interdependency to demonstrate how necessary relationships are to a boy's maturity. M. C.'s greatest possession is a forty-foot flagpole from which he can survey his family's land, Sara's Mountain. M. C.'s mother tells him that the flagpole is a signifier to M. C.'s father of all the gravestones that he removed from the family cemetery when M. C.'s mother wanted the yard cleared for her children to play in. She tells her son, "The pole is the marker for all of the dead" (106). Once M. C. discovers this fact, it seems to change the nature of the pole. No longer a simple phallic symbol marking a boy's sense of power, the pole becomes a symbol of the strength that knowledge of one's ancestry can give.[2]

M. C.'s family takes great pride in their ownership of Sara's Mountain, but they discriminate against another African American family who lives in the hills, the Killburns. Although M. C. dwells on how different the Higginses and the Killburns look, the greatest difference between the two families is actually their attitude toward the land. The Higginses feel that freedom is integral to the ownership of land because M. C.'s great-great-grandmother Sara obtained the land after she escaped from slavery. All of M. C.'s ancestors since Sara's time are buried on the mountain, so Mr. Higgins refuses to leave, even though waste material from strip mining threatens to obliterate the family's home. Mr. Higgins defines his identity in relationship to his ownership of the mountain: "'It's a *feeling*,' Jones [Mr. Higgins] said. 'Like, to think a solid piece of something big belongs to you. To your father, and his, too.' Jones rubbed and twisted his hands, as if they ached him. 'And you to it, for a long kind of time'" (77). For Mr. Higgins, ownership represents connection to the past and to the future.

But for Mr. Killburn, who is also the father of M. C.'s best friend, ownership is impossible. "Soil is body," he tells M. C. and a girl he has just met named Luhretta Outlaw. "We don't own nothing of it. We just caretakers, here to be of service" (229). After explaining that the Killburns are vegetarians because they believe that vegetables are part of the human body, as are all living things, Mr. Killburn emphasizes interrelationships. The contrast between Mr. Killburn's and Mr. Higgins's attitudes toward ownership creates a conflict that M. C. must resolve.

The Killburns live in an enclave that has no yard because every available space of land is planted with vegetables. To connect their houses to each other, the members of the enclave have constructed an elaborate rope ladder suspended above the vegetable garden. Described as a cobweb (218), the rope ladder evokes the cobweb imagery of interpersonal relationships that Gilligan describes, although here, both males and females partake of a morality of interconnectedness. It also seems significant that the ladder runs not vertically as ladders normally do, but horizontally, creating equality rather than hierarchies. When someone describes the ladder as a cobweb, Mr. Killburn disagrees and calls it an eye, but one that is "better than any old eye. Bigger. *A eye* of Gawd" (230).

From Mr. Killburn, M. C. learns to think of ownership as stewardship. And as a steward, he is able to devise a plan to save his family's home. Anita Moss points out that M. C. develops this plan as a result of being exposed to a variety of feminist moral codes:

> After he encounters both New Woman in the person of young Luhretta Outlaw and the traditional matriarchal values on Killburn Mound, M. C. acquires a more balanced and integrated sense of self—what some feminist critics have called "the androgynous self." He seems content to make home safe for every member of the family through his humble act of building a wall, rather than attempting to dominate the entire mountain on his forty-foot pole in the difficult patriarchal role of "M. C. Higgins, the Great." It is this kind of aggressive patriarchy—M.C. the Hunter, the conqueror of the earth—that, in its most extreme form, has resulted in the rape of the mountain by strip mining. ("Frontiers" 25)

Nodelman disagrees with Moss's assertion that M. C. becomes more androgynous. He claims:

> If the ending of *M. C. Higgins* has positive value, if it is a sane and healthy book, it is so because it views traditional masculinity from within what has traditionally been viewed as a feminine perspective—and rightly finds it lacking: it is no accident that M. C. erect on his pole is actually impotent, unable to do anything but go around in circles. . . . The novel is less androgynous, less a blending of traditional masculine and feminine values than a healthy act of replacing a clearly deficient, dangerously paternalistic, and traditionally masculine view of individuality with a view of selfhood defined by responsibility and respect that in traditional terms seems weakly effeminate. ("Children's Literature" 34)

Ultimately, both critics seem to be arguing that what makes *M. C. Higgins the Great* good is the way the novel balances negative stereotypes of masculinity with positive stereotypes of femininity. As a result, Hamilton could be accused of essentializing, but she redeems herself by having two male characters, M. C. and his father, embrace a community-oriented ethos. Hamilton makes clear that women don't hold a monopoly on valuing community.

The wall that M. C. builds to protect himself and his family is constructed from paraphernalia lying around the family's yard. M. C. digs it up with the hunting knife that Luhretta has given him; he is using the gift of the liberated feminist to build rather than to kill. M. C.'s energy inspires the rest of his family to help him, so the project becomes a community effort. But the most significant contribution to the wall comes from M. C.'s father when he donates the gravestones from the family cemetery to the wall, using the past to protect the future. And as a symbol, the gravestones in the wall represent the connections, the interrelationships, between generations.

M. C. has been conscious throughout the book of the importance of interrelationships. His mother, Banina, describes living on the mountain with her family as "all together. All apart. But all" (133). For Banina, individuality matters, but community matters more. This is ultimately what makes M. C. great; not his dominance over the land and the people on it but his recognition and appreciation of the people who live with him and those who have lived before him.[3]

HETEROSEXUAL RELATIONSHIPS

Heterosexual relationships have been problematic in adolescent literature since the genre was formalized by Angie's rejection of the lower-class Jack in the denouement of Maureen Daly's *Seventeenth Summer* (1942).[4] Girls in young adult novels often learn to validate themselves through a male's opinion, as Angie does in *Seventeenth Summer*, or they sacrifice their strength to a male, as Lorraine does in Paul Zindel's *The Pigman* (1968), or they are objectified, as they are in Robert Cormier's *The Chocolate War* (1974). Young adult novels influenced by the different forms of feminism, however, make overt efforts to overcome the paradigm of the voiceless female in adolescent literature. Two examples serve to illustrate my point: the young women in Janet Lunn's *Shadow in Hawthorn Bay* (1986) and Barbara Wersba's *Love Is the Crooked Thing* refuse to be victimized by heterosexual love.

Janet Lunn explicitly deconstructs the paradigm of the dependent female in a heterosexual relationship that supplants all others in *Shadow in Hawthorn Bay*. Mary, a telepathic adolescent, leaves her home in Ireland when she hears her beloved, Duncan, calling her from Canada, where he has emigrated. Mary suffers the travails common to most pioneers in the nineteenth-century Canadian wilderness, but when she arrives at Hawthorn Bay, she discovers that Duncan has already died. Grief-stricken and impoverished, Mary works to earn her return passage home. Luke, the son of one of the local settlers, falls in love with the headstrong Mary, but she will not allow his advances because she is still so in love with the memory of Duncan.

Mary settles in Duncan's old house on the shores of Hawthorn Bay despite the disapproval of her neighbors. She eventually harbors Henry, Luke's younger brother, who has fled his abusive home. Both Mary and Henry notice something ominous about the bay; a certain shaded patch of the water seems to entice them to drown themselves. Eventually Mary realizes that the shadow in the bay is the ghost of Duncan, who drowned himself there. She exorcises herself of Duncan's power over her in an apostrophe to him: "When you wanted to die, then you called. You wanted me to die with you. . . . Alive and dead, you were like a shadow. And I thought I could not manage life without you. I thought you were so strong because you were beautiful and exciting. Time was I would follow you anywhere. . . . But not into that other world I would not follow. Duncan, it was not strong to drown yourself so, it was evil to come after me" (201). Mary decides to marry Luke, so the book does not communicate that solitary independence is preferable to interdependence. In that sense, Lunn refuses to allow her protagonist to enter the Huckleberry Finn archetype: lighting off in solitude is no feminist resolution. *Shadow in Hawthorn Bay* is also a triumph of unconditional love over conditional love. Luke understands and cherishes Mary as she is and in ways that Duncan never could. The text affirms the importance of heterosexual relationships that allow women to be strong and self-fulfilled.

Barbara Wersba's *Fat: A Love Story* (1987) also explores the nuances of heterosexual relationships. *Fat* is Rita Formica's story of how she falls in love with an older man named Arnold Bromberg, who is mildly eccentric. Part of their love affair involves Rita's demonstrating her independence to her parents, who are completely demoralized by Rita and Arnold's affair. Rita also loses some of her closeness to her girlfriend Corry because she devotes so much time to Arnold. But the story is important for demonstrating two people in love who accept each other despite their differences: Arnold understands Rita's weight problem because he is also overweight, and Rita understands Arnold's passion for poetry and organ playing because she, as a budding writer, also considers herself an artist.

The sequel, *Love Is the Crooked Thing*, is even richer in feminist overtones than *Fat: A Love Story*. The story opens with Arnold finally convinced by Rita's parents that his love for Rita is inappropriate, so he leaves unannounced for Europe. When Rita decides she needs to earn money to go to Europe and find her lover, she approaches the pulp romance writer Doris Morris and asks to work in her stable. Doris agrees, and the job turns into one that gives Rita some of the experience as a writer that she has needed. Doris becomes a mentor for Rita both artistically and emotionally; the older woman advises the seventeen year old to go to Zurich and lends her the money to do so. Rita's friend Corry agrees to cover for Rita as she flies to Zurich; she tells her parents she is spending the weekend with Corry.

As it turns out, Rita's bonds with Doris and Corry are more lasting than her bond with Arnold, for when she gets to Zurich she discovers that although Arnold still loves her, he is not willing to make the sacrifices necessary for them to have a continuing relationship. Arnold tells her he is still too old for her and will never have a steady enough job to support her; he also points out that her parents will never approve. Rita does not accept his excuses, though. She tells him: "Our problem isn't my age, or your income. And our problem isn't my parents, either. Our problem is simply that you're a confirmed bachelor, Arnold Bromberg, who is scared as hell of responsibility. . . . You pursued me because I was too young, and the next woman you love will probably be all wrong too. However. When you get over this childishness, I, Rita, will be waiting for you" (162). On the flight home, wondering what she will do with herself, Rita recognizes that she has been "*too* desperate, too needy," and she tells herself, "And you depended on Arnold to make you thin. The only person who can make you thin, kiddo, is you" (164). In an epiphanic moment, she sees that her affair with Arnold has provided her with the material for the romantic novel she has always wanted to write. Once she is strong enough to walk away from a weak man, she finally gains the artistic productivity she has sought. Thus, Rita follows the basic paradigm for the feminist *Künstlerroman*: she is secure in her art without sacrificing her self by the novel's end.

Before the novel ends, Rita also makes some striking generalizations: "I closed my eyes and thought about men. Men who just wanted sex . . . and men who were romantics, like Arnold—but who didn't want to get trapped—and then I thought about men like my father, who get married and support families and wind up drinking too much" (165). Rita finally understands that the way our culture socializes men makes it impossible for them to be the sort of fairy-tale figure that she has sought, the romantic hero from a pulp romance.

When she arrives home, she greets her mother in the kitchen and makes amends for the tension between them, and the two begin to renew their relationship by eating veal stew and watching *Wuthering Heights*. That the novel concludes this way, with Rita's renewing her bond with her mother and with Rita's friendships with Doris Morris and her girlfriend Corry remaining intact, communicates that honest emotional bonds with other females will last longer than shallow sexual bonds with men.

Any number of feminist adolescent novels demonstrate the paradigm of a young woman who is empowered despite being engaged in a heterosexual relationship. The novels in Voigt's fantasy trilogy, *Jackaroo* (1985), *On Fortune's Wheel*, and *The Wings of a Falcon* (1990), all conclude with an independent woman who retains her integrity in a heterosexual relationship.[5] Virginia Hamilton's *A White Romance* demonstrates an adolescent girl's growing awareness of the difference between being repressed in a sexist relationship and being liberated in a nonsexist one. Ho's *Rice without Rain*, Taylor's *The Road to Memphis*, Katherine Paterson's *Lyddie*, and Matas's *The Burning Time* also show female characters with integrity who scrutinize what it means for women to enter into heterosexual relationships.

FEMALE BONDS

Bonds between females have always existed in children's literature, but they are often depicted as being less important than heterosexual relationships. Jo and her sisters sacrifice their sororal community for love of men; Cinderella and her sisters compete for a man's attention, as do friends in *A Tree Grows in Brooklyn*. Feminist children's novels, however, often rewrite the Freudian model of women competing for a man's love to explore the many facets of female/female relationships that can bring strength to the women and girls involved. Whether the female bonding takes place in friendships, real or surrogate sisterhoods, lesbian relationships, or mother/daughter relationships, its purpose in these texts is to explore female relationships as a metaphor for community. And within the metaphorical community, female protagonists are free to explore their subjectivity and engage their agency and their voices.

One of the most important feminist novels in this regard is *Annie on My Mind* (1982) by Nancy Garden, a love story about the romance between Liza Winthrop and Annie Kenyon. The counterplot parallels the girls' relationship with another lesbian couple: two teachers at Liza's school get fired for their lesbianism. Liza feels responsible for their dismissal because she and Annie are the reason the school has discovered the older women's lesbianism, so for six months she distances herself from her lover. But what Liza eventually learns from Ms. Widmer and Ms. Stevenson is to continue to love Annie, for "what matters is the truth of loving, of two people finding each other" (229). Ms. Stevenson has often told Liza that the truth shall set her free, and Liza does feel set free when she overcomes feeling responsible for hurting other people—her family, her teachers, her friends—because of her lesbianism. Liza and Annie renew their relationship at the end of the narrative. The reader is left to believe that they will be able to fulfill their hope of living without hiding, as Annie puts it, "the best part of my life, of myself" from themselves or their society (154).

The story contains an embedded narrative structure. The framing tale is narrated in the third person as Liza, now a freshman at MIT, remembers the previous year. Using pouring rain to represent the narrator's anguish, tears, and tortured memories, the framing tale seems intentionally clichéd in places. But in the embedded narrative Liza's voice is first person and less trite; she claims a strong narrative position as she tells how she met and fell in love with Annie. The alternations in voice achieve a number of effects. Liza's voice is both specific to her in the first person and universalized as the voice of the lover in the third person; her persona seems at times immediate and at other times more removed. The framing tale also heightens the romance of the novel, clearly attempting to situate the text within the genre of the romance novel, even though that genre is generally heterosexist. By incorporating standard devices from romance novels into her lesbian revision of the genre, Garden appropriates the genre in an act that is at once revisionary and reconciliatory. The text of *Annie on My Mind* implies repeatedly that lesbianism is just another facet of human love, and the use of the genre-dependent narrative frame is one more technique that Garden uses to communicate that message.

Moreover, since the telling of the tale is critical to Liza's healing, the process of narrative creation becomes symbolic of strength. Liza does not reach out to Annie until she has retold their story, until she has (re)created and (re)generated the narrative of their love. In the chapters that follow, I focus on the creation of narrativity as a source of female self-definition and community formation, but here I think it is specifically important as a tool of female bonding: Liza wants the type of connection with Annie that she describes Ms. Widmer and Ms. Stevenson sharing, and she uses her storytelling to establish that bond.

Liza's storytelling generates another level of female bonding, however, for the text itself represents a feminist, Nancy Garden, trying to connect with female readers to communicate that lesbianism is not only acceptable, but it can also be beautiful. Several passages give the book a self-help flavor: most notably, Plato's explanation of homosexuality in chapter 9 and the bibliography of books about lesbianism incorporated into chapter 13. This is understandable, given the text's agenda. Garden wants to reassure her reader, to communicate with her, and to establish a relationship, a community. Thus, *Annie on My Mind* articulates a central issue of female bonds in feminist children's and adolescent novels: female community established between the characters and between the author and reader can provide a source of empowerment like no other.

The primacy of female friendship also underscores Cynthia Voigt's *Tell Me If the Lovers Are Losers* (1982). A school story set in 1961 about three roommates at Stanton College, the story explores the dynamics between three distinctly different personalities and how they affect each other's lives. The book is narrated primarily through the consciousness of Ann, an East Coast "stupid preppy bitch," as Niki, her obnoxious, athletic roommate from California, characterizes her (87). Hildy, on scholarship from North Dakota, is a stolid girl, set in her conservative opinions and largely unflappable. The three freshman develop a sense of camaraderie as they strive to defeat the sophomore team at the school's volleyball tournament.

The three roommates often do not understand each other's values, as, for instance, when Niki reveals that her parents are divorced and Hildy condemns Niki's mother. Niki defends her mother, but Hildy insists that Niki's mother has been wrong to abandon her child. Hildy insists so long that cracks eventually begin to appear in Niki's attempts to argue as a feminist; she thinks that if she were a boy her mother might have stayed (86). Niki's inconsistency leaves an ambiguity for the reader to interpret: both Niki's inconsistency and Hildy's dogmatism are wrong. The disagreement, however, characterizes the central difference between the two girls. Hildy interprets everything in categorical imperatives as either right or wrong, and Niki believes that winning is what makes people right. The text critiques both stances.

When Niki and Ann discover that Hildy is nearsighted, they arrange a way to buy eyeglasses for her so that she will not know that they have extended charity to her. Ann eventually starts putting Hildy's glasses on for fun, enjoying how the lenses distort everything she sees through them. She comes to think of them as a new way to "assimilate . . . information" (186). Ann even begins to wear the glasses while she watches the volleyball games. The glasses are clearly a symbol of both girls' changing subjectivity: without them, Hildy cannot see well enough to do her schoolwork, but she plays better volleyball without them. For Hildy, they represent the refinement school is offering her, new ways of thinking and new ways of perceiving herself, but she still needs to be able to remove these new lenses before she can perform the tasks she was successful at (like volleyball) before she ever came to school. For Ann, the glasses are a way to better understand someone else's subject position(s). But it bothers her that whenever she asks Hildy how she perceives her, Ann, without the glasses on, Hildy cannot describe what she sees (186, 210).

Niki eventually condemns Hildy for accepting the school's scholarship when she plans to leave in a year to return to North Dakota to get married. After their fight, Hildy stops wearing her glasses, which she thinks of as something she has bought with the school's money, and as a result she is killed while riding her bicycle because she fails to see a swerving car. Niki experiences her grief as a loss; she is a lover who has lost. But the grief Niki and Ann share allows them to become deeper friends. Niki asks Ann: "Are we going to be friends after all? I mean, friends—not hello-how-are-you people. I'd like that, Annie, and I'll tell you why. Might as well now I've started. *Because you've got a good eye for the true thing*, for excellence. Hildy said. So, *see*, if we were friends—if you were my friend it might mean I was the true thing" (239, emphasis added). Ann, who has been wearing Hildy's glasses to better understand the truth, is moved that Hildy considered her to be someone with true moral vision. The book closes with Ann and Niki's friendship firmly intact. But Ann's perception of life has been forever changed: "Ann always kept Hildy's glasses and sometimes wore them, as she had before. Grief remained in her, intractable. Memory also remained and grew golden. In time. She had Hildy's glasses and could see through them. She knew better than to forget, or want to. After Hildy's life, her death, no blind peace" (241). Ann's preppie world has been shattered, but her understanding of life has been enriched by her friendship with these two unusual girls.

Rosa Guy's *The Friends* (1973) is another clear tribute to the importance of female friendship as girls mature into women. The first-person narrator, Phyllisia, tells the story of how she becomes friends with Edith Jackson, a girl whom Phyllisia initially dislikes. Edith is untidy, her clothes are disheveled, and she is oblivious to her teacher's antagonism (3). Edith is also oblivious to Phyllisia's indifference to her. Phyllisia's attitude stems from snobbery. Her father, Calvin, has emigrated from the West Indies to New York, where he owns what he leads his daughter to believe is a successful restaurant. He is obsessed with two things: controlling his restaurant and controlling his daughters. The whole story revolves around who has the right to control Phyllisia's life, she or her father.

Calvin firmly believes that his daughters belong to a better class than most of the people in their neighborhood. As a result of believing this herself, fourteen-year-old Phyllisia needs to overcome the classism in which her father has immersed her. This classism tinged with some intraracial bigotry informs the entire book, for it is the value that most controls Phyllisia until she learns better. Her friendship with Edith, however, emerges from two forms of adult pressure: their white teacher's bigoted abuse and Phyllisia's father's domineering control. In developing a covert friendship with someone these people in authority despise, Phyllisia sets herself up as a rebel against the system. She draws strength from defining herself as rejecting this system. The text of *The Friends* thus demonstrates female friendship as a form of sisterhood that exists in opposition to the strictures of any authority that would deny others power.

As Phyllisia's mother lies dying, she tells Phyllisia how classist she has been to Edith. But Phyllisia, immersed in her shame at Edith's class and her shame with herself for caring, still considers herself Edith's superior. Only after Phyllisia goes to her father's restaurant for the first time and realizes that it is little more than a greasy spoon owned by a man struggling to make ends meet, only after she knows that her father's restaurant is hardly the well-cultured and lucrative place she had imagined does she recognize how deeply Calvin's classism has infected her. She finally goes to Edith, who is about to be sent to an orphanage with her sisters, and declares her permanent loyalty to Edith: "Don't ever say again you don't have anybody. You have me. And you'll have me as long as I live" (196). This time, the bond of the friendship is permanent because it comes from something more than rebellion: it grows out of respect.

The friendship gives Phyllisia the strength to face her father finally, rather than deceiving him as she has done throughout the book. She refuses to be sent back to the West Indies on the grounds that "I promised my friend that I would come to see her every week while she is in the orphanage" (199). She convinces her father that they are partially responsible for Edith's condition because they have been too class-conscious to help her, and she promises her father that she will not be "spiteful" to him anymore (201). But the words that convince Calvin to let her stay in New York seem to be the most honest she utters in the whole book: "'I'm much older today than I was yesterday.' He looked at me strangely. His entire face underwent a change and I knew that for the first time he was regarding me as a person, apart from himself" (201). Once Phyllisia confronts her father with the self-reliance that a friendship based on love has given her, he can finally perceive her as something other than an object or a possession. More than providing just a means to fight repressive authority, then, friendship in Guy's *The Friends* is a source of self-authorization from which girls can gain strength.

Katherine Paterson's *Lyddie* is a novel set in the 1840s about friendship, sisterhood, and friendships that turn into sisterhoods. Like Dicey Tillerman in Voigt's *The Homecoming* (1981), Lyddie is left with the care of her younger siblings because her father has wandered off and her mother has gone insane. Lyddie seeks work at the mills in Lowell, but she is too intent on saving money in order to reunite her family to have time to respond to the overtures of friendship from the various girls she meets. At this stage of her development, Lyddie is basically antifeminist. Eventually, however, Lyddie learns that her only hope in bettering her working conditions and her life resides in making friends, in developing a sense of community with other women, and ultimately in becoming a feminist.

Four girls play significant roles in changing Lyddie. One of her roommates, Betsy, teaches her to read and to aspire to seek further education. Another mill worker, Diana, teaches Lyddie to have self-respect. When Lyddie's younger sister Rachel comes to live with her in Lowell for a while, Lyddie begins to overcome some of her stinginess. Rachel denies that she "is a cheap old spinster" and tells Lyddie, "You're the best sister in the world!" (139). Rachel's adoration of Lyddie thaws her penurious heart enough that she can even let go of her dream of reuniting her family. When her younger brother and Rachel are offered a chance at being adopted by kindhearted people, Lyddie allows them to go. She has learned to love so freely that she wants what is best for Rachel and Charlie, not what is best for herself. After Rachel leaves, Lyddie compensates for her loneliness by forming a relationship with another young woman, Brigid. Lyddie teaches Brigid to read as Betsy once taught her, and Lyddie protects the younger worker from the sexual harassment of their overseer.[6]

After she is fired for confronting the overseer, Lyddie decides to journey to Oberlin, where Betsy has told her that women are admitted to college. Even when a neighbor offers to marry her and help her set up housekeeping in her old home, Lyddie remains determined to get an education. Betsy, Diana, and Brigid have inspired too much of a sense of community in Lyddie for her to settle immediately into a heterosexual relationship on an isolated farm. But since Lyddie has learned the importance of interdependency, she leaves herself the possibility of marriage, glad that the man who has proposed to her is so open-minded, and she continues her quest to be her own person. But she never would have discovered her own strength had she not had a nurturing female community within which to develop.

In confirming the importance of interrelationships, feminist authors establish a relationship that creates another community: one with their readers. For the feminist reader, reading a feminist text is an exercise in immersing herself or himself within a community of women. Patrocinio Schweickart comments on the female community engendered by feminist reading:

> Mainstream reader-response theories are preoccupied with issues of control and partition—how to distinguish the contribution of the author/text from the contribution of the reader. In the dialectic of communication informing the relationship between the feminist reader and the female author/text, the central issue is not of control or partition, but of managing the contradictory implications of the desire for relationship (one must maintain a minimal distance from the other) and the desire for intimacy, up to and including a symbiotic merger with the other. (55)

Schweickart investigates the implications of the reading subject's role as she reads: is she displaced by the characters who constitute the textual subject or not? Schweickart maintains that feminist reading requires the reader to be simultaneously aware of her displacement by the text and of her own connection to it. Schweickart's definition of feminist reader response resides in the necessity of there being an interconnection between the writer and the reader. Thus, when an author such as Garden or Wersba or Guy attempts to reach the reading subject, the author makes it possible for the text to create a connection between two subjects rather than a displacement of one by the other. That author has then created a feminist text that privileges feminist reading.

Following what Schweickart says, we can speculate about the implications of interrelationships in feminist children's novels as a whole. Almost every feminist children's text shows some sort of community being built, and almost every feminist children's text allows for the connection of one human (the author) with another (the reader). What really matters, then, about the focus on relationships in feminist children's novels is the way these novels demonstrate people interacting, gaining strength from each other, and being strong in their relationships. All the characters I have discussed in this chapter rely on their own unique voices to foster their interrelationships. Moreover, in writing these texts, Cynthia Rylant, Virginia Hamilton, Janet Lunn, Barbara Wersba, Nancy Garden, Cynthia Voigt, Rosa Guy, and Katherine Paterson have used their own voices to offer themselves to readers so that another type of bond occurs. Readers of these novels experience not only the communities that Summer and M. C. cherish and the relationships that sustain Liza and Phyllisia; they also experience a bond with the community of feminist writers. Readers of feminist children's novels thus participate actively in a vital feminist community.

7. REFUTING FREUD:

MOTHER/DAUGHTER

RELATIONSHIPS

In chapter 6, I investigated the implications of community as an arena in which the child or adolescent protagonist could explore her voice within different types of inter-relationships. The most complex form of relationship in feminist literature, however, seems to be the mother/daughter relationship, for that is the primary relationship for many girls. Adrienne Rich notes that mother-and-daughterhood existed long before cultural constructs of sisterhood did, and that the mother/daughter relationship, at various times both blown out of proportion and not given enough attention, "is the great unwritten story" (*Of Woman Born* 225). She further notes that "the loss of the daughter to the mother, the mother to the daughter, is the essential female tragedy. We acknowledge Lear (father-daughter split), Hamlet (son and mother), and Oedipus (son and mother) as great embodiments of the human tragedy; but there is no presently enduring recognition of mother-daughter passion and rapture" (237). Although Jo loves her mother passionately in *Little Women*, few other classics of children's literature demonstrate mother/daughter bonds at all, much less strong, positive ones. Jamaica Kincaid's *Annie John* (1983) is perhaps the closest recent text that tries to breach this gap: Annie lives rapturously with her mother until she discovers her parents having sex. The girl's discovery of sex leads to her departure from the Garden of Eden: Annie no longer lives in paradisiacal harmony with her mother. Roni Natov analyzes Kincaid's *Annie John* as a Lacanian story; Annie's childhood naïveté marks a pre-Oedipal innocence that can no longer exist once she becomes aware of her father as the figure who splits her from her imaginary oneness with her mother.[1] Natov's work delineates for feminists the strength that can adhere to a mother/daughter relationship that is not corrupted by classically Freudian competitions for male attention, but her work focuses on the daughter's subject position, as many feminist critiques tend to do, in a way that virtually ignores the maternal subject position.

Barbara Johnson suggests three possibilities wherein pre-Oedipal paradigms, such as the one used by Natov, could be interpreted as a positive rather than as a regressive aspect of growing up (142). First, she believes more than simple autonomy from the mother should be used as a mark of maturity. Mothering, she says, should be viewed as only one of a number of possible "maturational models" (143). Second, she perceives the Oedipal model as needlessly favoring the point of view of a child who must necessarily be egotistical. When we interpret literature through a Freudian lens, we necessarily focus more on the child/Oedipus figure than on the parent figure, and since childhood is a necessarily ego-centered time, Freudian readings invariably result in readings that focus on the child at the expense of the adult, especially the mother. And third, Johnson advocates analyzing the maternal figure "as the subject of discourse rather than as the source of life or the object of desire and anger" (143).

Children's literature as a field of study has had some success in regard to at least the last of these three suggestions, for several studies exist that share a goal with this chapter: they investigate maternal subjectivities within literary discourse. In fact, among children's literature critics, the mother/daughter relationship is problematized more than any other facet of female-female relationships, perhaps because (rightly or wrongly) the mother stands in our culture as the representative of female adulthood for children. For example, Mitzi Myers investigates the implications of the power of mothers and surrogate mothers in Georgian children's books in her essay "Impeccable

Governesses, Rational Dames, and Moral Mothers." Myers concludes that for women such as Wollstonecraft, the creation of "benign and powerful maternal governance and good girlhood reflect[s] both female fantasies and real cultural change. On the one hand, they read nurture as power, showing a decided preference for maturity over the childishness male preceptors recommend to women. . . . On the other hand . . . [they] encode complex social messages" (54–55). Anita Clair Fellman explores a similar dynamic between the strength of nurturing and the benefits of being nurtured in the actual mother/daughter relationship between Laura Ingalls Wilder and her daughter in "Laura Ingalls Wilder and Rose Wilder Lane: The Politics of a Mother-Daughter Relationship." Both Myers and Fellman imply that the subject positions of mothers and of daughters have significance in the creation of fiction.

In the most comprehensive study to date of the mother/daughter relationship as it is manifested in picture books, Adrienne Kertzer explores the silencing of the mother in picture books. Kertzer analyzes the multiplicity of techniques used to suppress mothers' voices in picture books. Her thesis, that mothers' voices are silenced in ways that the voices of other adults are not in picture books (159), is relevant to an investigation of mother/daughter relationships in children's novels. Kertzer speculates that mothers' voices are marginalized as a result of the cult of perfect motherhood and as a result of the desire to promote children's points of view in children's literature (159–60). Kertzer then deconstructs a central irony of the image of the mother in picture books: mothers read picture books to their children that show mothers to be silent (159).

These points are germane to children's novels, for interestingly enough, the voice of the mother is more often heard in contemporary children's novels than it is in picture books. That this phenomenon coincides with the time that the child is no longer dependent on her mother to read to her is interesting; it indicates that children can accept strong literary mothers as they grow older and become more sure of their own voices. This is not to imply, however, that children's novels are replete with maternal voices, for this is far from the case. Whether feminist or otherwise, more children's novels omit maternal subjectivities than include them. Myers offers an explanation for the weakness of maternal voices in Georgian children's fictions when she suggests that the absence may be a result of the authors' having wished to have been better mothered themselves (54). Applied to recent American children's fiction, Myers's speculation could be extended as a commentary on the desires of currently publishing women in the field: lacking strong artistic mother/mentors, they transfer their own motherlessness to their writing so that their female characters are also motherless. While this tendency has fit conveniently into the commonplace of children's literature that parents must be absent from the narrative in order for the child characters to have adventures and to explore on their own, it seems that as feminism has influenced the culture, stronger mother/daughter relationships have begun to infiltrate the children's novel.

Mother/daughter relationships take two predominant forms in children's and adolescent novels: those traditional narratives that allow for the daughter to achieve independence from her mother in the classically Oedipal manner that Nancy Friday describes in *My Mother/My Self*, and those less traditional and less Freudian ones that allow the daughter to mature without necessarily breaking from her mother. While the former focuses on the daughters' strength, the latter category, including Pam Conrad's *Prairie Songs* (1985) and Virginia Hamilton's *Plain City* (1993), allows both mothers and daughters to be strong. Some novels in this latter category, moreover, use narrative structure to explore positive mother/daughter relationships in a pattern that I identify in the final section of this chapter.

The weakest of the Freudian rebellious-daughter novels, however, portray mothers as evil beings whose stifling presence must be escaped in order for the misunderstood daughter to develop fully. The mothers in these books are often one-dimensional: they are controlling, manipulative, and little more. I am not denying that plenty of overbearing, manipulative mothers have caused plenty of daughters to rebel in actuality, but books like M. E. Kerr's *Dinkey Hocker Shoots Smack* (1972) and Judy Blume's *Deenie* (1973) are reductive in their portraits of mothers. Rarely do books in this genre explore why it is that the controlling mother is a recognizable pattern in our culture; rarely do they investigate why the mother specifically being maligned is herself so maladjusted.[2]

THE FREUDIAN MOTHER/DAUGHTER PLOT

The best example that I have found of a book in this genre that explores the controlling mother's motivations is Crescent Dragonwagon's roman à clef, *The Year It Rained* (1985).[3] Dragonwagon is overtly committed to a feminist agenda: Elizabeth Stein, the narrator of the text, mocks herself for enjoying sexist romantic comedies (25), and she wishes *Ms.* would write an exposé on her school's sexual double standards (200). Elizabeth can also see that despite her mother's commitment to gender equality with her husband early in their marriage, their ideals have never been realized. Her mother works on the couch unless her husband is home; then he gets the couch and she works in a chair. More important and less symbolic, Elizabeth's mother has always wanted to be a writer but has never had time to be one because she has been too busy supporting the family so that her husband can be free to write.

Elizabeth is obsessed with her mother, whom she calls Katherine. Elizabeth is specifically fixated on how perfect her mother is and how many people wish Katherine were their mother. The novel opens, "I have the mother everyone wants," and the sentiment is repeated throughout the text. Katherine is a very controlled woman who is a successful editor of children's books. She never lets her feelings show, but she is always aware of other people's feelings. Her kindness is one way she controls Elizabeth; Elizabeth feels terrible if she causes her mother pain. Yet Elizabeth suffers from a biochemically based schizophrenia and has attempted suicide three times. After each attempt, her mother has grown kinder and more protective so that Elizabeth feels smothered.

Elizabeth's greatest desire is to be a writer, but she feels stifled because of her mother's keen interest and because of her mother's failure to pursue writing herself. It is as if Elizabeth is afraid to succeed where her mother has failed. Elizabeth's moment of transcendence, which she actually calls an "epiphany" (213), comes when she decides to pursue her dream of writing despite her mother. It is this transcendence that keeps *The Year It Rained* from being more than just another derivative of *The Bell Jar*. It is also this epiphany that Roger Sutton completely misses when he says of Elizabeth that she "remain[s] as self-centered and self-important" as she was at the novel's opening (43). It is no surprise to me that Sutton misses the novel's feminist transcendence; throughout his masculinist review, he keeps claiming that he wants to "smack" Elizabeth (43).

Elizabeth experiences her epiphany at a poetry reading when she talks to the poet. She suddenly understands that the woman is happy because she is "a person living a life of self-understanding" (205). As Elizabeth hugs the poet good-bye, she thinks about a time as a child when she impulsively hugged a musician whose music touched her soul:

> Then I hadn't had words; now I had them but knew their limits. Then, I was a child, reaching toward a grown man, a magic man who picked me up, hard, firm, black, tall. Now I was a woman, hugging a woman, hugging someone, something, that was like me: soft, white, rounded, same size, same height. Both of our feet were on the ground, we were celebrating the picking up of ourselves, by ourselves, our survival, our writing—hers already begun, mine still to be, yet also, in its way, already begun.
> Different and identical, full circle. (208)

The concept of circularity has been important to Elizabeth throughout the text, but here it gains significance as a feminist symbol, as a sign of sharing, equality, and sisterhood. The circularity also ties into the narrative structure of the novel, which has been constructed by means of a pastiche of flashbacks and tangents that inevitably return to Elizabeth's inability to grow until she can come to terms with her mother's perfection. Elizabeth overcomes her writer's block by refusing to be her mother anymore when she decides that if her mother truly wanted to write, "she would" (205). Elizabeth then begins to write about the past year in her life to help her make sense of it, so the novel ends with the sort of circular narrative device that *The Outsiders* and *It All Began with Jane Eyre* use; the end of the narrative is its beginning.

Part of Elizabeth's growth has been to recognize that her mother is responsible for her own fears and feelings of guilt. But Elizabeth's growth does not preclude her having a relationship with her mother. The book ends with Elizabeth and Katherine's shared excitement that Elizabeth has finally done something for herself: she has bought herself a red shirt, symbolic of the strength she had as a child when she loved red and symbolic also of her separation from her mother, whose favorite colors are green and blue. Katherine rejoices at Elizabeth's choice because, as Elizabeth notes, her mother sees it as a sign that Elizabeth has hope for the future. Katherine offers her daughter "a bite to eat," evoking the nurturance often associated with motherhood. Elizabeth agrees to share the communal meal with her, but only after she has done something for herself: she looks up the meaning of the word "epiphany" (213). *The Year It Rained* concludes with a bond between Elizabeth and her mother, but it is a bond that recognizes their differences and validates their separation.

THE ANTI-FREUDIAN MOTHER/DAUGHTER PLOT

In Pam Conrad's *Prairie Songs*, Clara Downing provides the sort of positive nurturance for her daughter, Louisa, that does not require the daughter to separate from her mother, so the book fits the second paradigm of mother/daughter relationships in children's novels. The story revolves around Louisa's growing to understand the relationship between maternity and death, and as a result, images evoking life and death recur throughout the text. The Downings are pioneers on the Nebraska prairie who are pleased that a doctor and his wife have agreed to settle in their farming community. When the Berrymans arrive, Mrs. Emmeline Berryman proves to be both frail and pregnant. Louisa is astounded that the woman wears a violet-colored dress, which encourages the reader to think of Emmeline as a fragile but beautiful flower. Louisa also notices that Emmeline's face after the long journey is "gray, like winter prairie grass before a bad storm" (9). The contrast Louisa has noticed between Emmeline's life-affirming dress and her death-foreshadowing face creates the tension in the book. Emmeline is too much like a "hothouse flower" to flourish in the harsh prairie (79).

Unlike Emmeline, Louisa finds beauty in the prairies, in the wide-open skies, in the strong grass, and in the prairie flowers. Emmeline, however, is unable to adapt. Their differences are typified by their taste in poetry. Emmeline's favorite Tennyson poem is the morbid "Mariana" because she identifies with the moaning Mariana's cry: "I am aweary, aweary. / I would that I were dead" (69). Louisa prefers the strength of "The Eagle; a Fragment" because she identifies with the image of the solitary bird "close to the sun in lonely lands" (69). The poetry readings occur while Emmeline teaches Louisa and her brother, Lester. Seeing their teacher on an almost daily basis, the two children sense the woman's increasing insanity. After her baby dies during childbirth, Emmeline becomes so crazy that when two Indians enter her soddie while her husband is away during a snowstorm, she runs screaming outside, where she freezes to death.

It is Clara, Louisa's mother, who thaws the body and prepares it for burial, just as it has been Clara who held Emmeline's infant as it died. Clara tries unsuccessfully to protect her children from seeing Emmeline's corpse, but she has never tried to hide the infant's death from them. Louisa and her brother are all too aware of infant mortality; only the year before their own little sister died. The contrast between the two women resides in their reactions to the deaths of their children: Emmeline despairs and dies; Clara mourns and lives.

Clara has passed some of her strength on to her daughter. If Louisa is a Tennysonian eagle instead of a Mariana, it is because she has learned her love of life and of the prairie from her mother. Clara refuses to let the prairie conquer her. She doggedly waters trees near her house, telling Emmeline before her death, "'I think everyone should have something in their life that they need to carry water to. Heavy water.' She smiled. 'And far'" (76). This attitude, that nurturance is both hard work and good for the soul, is what allows Clara to survive pioneer life. Clara's strength, love, and affirmation of her children make it possible for the whole family to triumph over the prairie. Clara is a maternal, life-giving woman.

Nurturing mothers appear often in the works of Virginia Hamilton: M. C. Higgins the Great, The Magical Adventures of Pretty Pearl, Justice and Her Brothers, and Arilla Sun Down (1976) all have positive mothers. And although the protagonist's relationship with her mother in Plain City is at times conflicted, the narrative affirms the mother/daughter relationship as essential to the character's growth. Buhlaire Sims's stated quest is a search for her father, whom she once believed was missing in action from the Vietnam War. An adult friend tells her that he is still alive, however, and Buhlaire begins the search that results more in a renewed relationship with her mother than anything else.

As with any archetypal quest for a parent wherein the quester searches for the parent as a metaphor for searching to understand her or his identity, Buhlaire wants to know more about herself. "*Who am I? Who am I?*" she asks (94). She feels self-conscious within the African American community because of her honey-colored skin and golden Rasta curls and because of being fatherless, so she thinks of herself as Other, as an "outside child" (15, 144). She is disturbed because she has no sense of her own "*back time*"; her mother and aunts will not tell her about her past or theirs because they say she would find it uninteresting (7). Buhlaire does not accept that explanation, nor does she accept her mother's theory that "*Children are mutants. You don't remember childhood, Buhlaire, 'cause young people are all-time mutating to the next stage of young'un. You can't remember from one day to the next because your brain is in a state of flux*" (31). Buhlaire mentally disproves her mother by thinking, "*Remember her telling me that*" (31).

Buhlaire is more accepting when someone describes growing up as a time when "things don't look the same each day" (27). Buhlaire agrees, "It's like, I wake up now, and I see things that were always there, only, I see them more, or something" (27). She is willing to acknowledge the mutability of life but not of her own memories, and she expresses her understanding of these changes with the visual metaphor "I see them more" to demonstrate her increasing sense of her own subjectivity. But it is only after Buhlaire has confronted both her parents that she recognizes her ability to claim the subject position.

Her confrontation with her mother revolves around the woman's continual absence. Bluezy Sims is a singer and exotic dancer, so she travels for a living. Buhlaire resents her mother's frequent absences: "Makes me feel worthless," she tells a friend (146). Bluezy's presence matters to Buhlaire, for she perceives her mother as the force that connects her extended family: "*we are pieces on a chain, not even touching. Mom is the chain's big center piece of gold*" (41).[4] Moreover, the presence and absence of mothers matter for many other characters in the text. A child in a homeless shelter embarrasses Buhlaire when he mistakes her for his missing mother (98–99), and her friend Grady mourns his missing mother (135). When Buhlaire finds her father, Junior Sims, he is living with other homeless people in a cavelike dwelling created by a highway overpass. As in *The Planet of Junior Brown* (1971), Junior's name emphasizes the text's focus on parents: Junior Sims has no name of his own; he bears only his father's. But when one woman in the cave claims to be Junior's mother, he rejects her assertions because he knows his own missing mother is white (121–22, 160). The homeless boy's, Grady's, and Junior's missing mothers reinforce how crucial Buhlaire's bond with her mother is.

The homeless boy, Grady, and Junior are all homeless at some time in their lives, but Buhlaire never has been because she has a mother who creates a home for her. In this sense, then, homelessness serves as a metaphor for motherlessness. Although the text's overt political agenda addresses homelessness, its implied agenda equates motherlessness with homelessness to develop a political implication about maternity: until women's lives are bettered so that they can be free to mother, the problem of homeless children will remain unsolved. And so, too, will the emotional ills that motherlessness metaphorically represents in this text.

The most poignant chapters in the novel are those in which Buhlaire most openly connects with her mother. Midway through the narrative, she goes to hear her mother perform. Bluezy opens with "Bridge over Troubled Water," a song about connection and union. She directs the song toward her daughter, and Buhlaire almost cries, she is so overwhelmed with emotion. Then Bluezy amazes her daughter by inviting her to sing a duet. They perform "Let It Be," and the text makes a point of including the verse from the Beatles' song that affirms maternity by proclaiming "Mother Mary's" wisdom (quoted on 79). Bluezy allows her daughter to finish the song with a solo, and their performance is greeted with a strong ovation. As she returns home from this exhilarating experience, Buhlaire thinks that having sung sets her apart from the rest of her family, as she notices her mother has also been set apart. *"What does it mean, that the music does that? I'll ask Mom one time"* (83). Music, as a shared bond that marks their difference from other people, is an aspect of being an "outside child" that Buhlaire actually values.

Buhlaire's identification with her mother is strong. So strong, in fact, that she feels ambivalence when people recognize her as Bluezy Sims's daughter. When Grady's father says, "Everybody knows

Bluezy's daughter," she is "surprised and pleased" and thinks "*I didn't know that. Someday, everybody's gonna know me by my first name, too*" (140). And she immediately tells him her name, simultaneously claiming identification with her mother and asserting her own sense of self.

Buhlaire's ability to so name herself, however, follows her encounter with her father in the cave. She and Grady go there with him after he rescues them from a blinding snow whiteout. The whiteout represents many things: that Buhlaire's vision of herself and others is still dim; that racial issues surround and terrify her; that although she feels isolated, she really is not. Once at the cave, Buhlaire is repulsed by her father's unkempt odor, and she is frightened by his flashes of insanity, but she loves him nevertheless. Seeing him reminds her that they used to play ball together, although he comments, "I swore you'd be a ball player, if you'da been a boy. Too bad" (117).

Buhlaire appreciates that he returns her "back time" to her: he fills a manila envelope with pictures of her and medals she has won. Buhlaire has forgotten about these mementos because he, apparently, has routinely entered her house and stolen them. As he tells her, "I had a right to you!" (129). Buhlaire misinterprets her father's attempts to possess her: she tells her mother, "He took the pictures and stuff because he wanted me with him. See? He wanted me to pay attention to him" (156). Even though she attributes higher motives to her father than he deserves, this return of her "back time" enables the girl to perceive herself differently, even if it takes awhile for her to perceive her mother and father clearly.

Buhlaire generously gives $200, half her savings, to her father. But she decides that she will not try to live with him as she had hoped because she recognizes that she could never enjoy his lifestyle. She eventually understands what her mother points out: "he loved the idea of you," even if he was incapable of staying home to actually love her (168). Nevertheless, Buhlaire's encounter with her father has completely changed her self-perception. She still thinks of herself as an "outside child," but she gives new significance to the words: "*I am like my dad, can't stand the indoors for long. Have to stride the land. Just an outside child!*" (169). Earlier, Buhlaire has gotten mad at Grady for "*signifying at me*" (36), but now she does it herself. Henry Louis Gates Jr. cites the importance of signifying as an African

American linguistic practice: by signifying, which is creating a double meaning with an "indirect intent" and a "metaphorical reference," Buhlaire can use words to gain power in her own life (85).[5]

Indeed, her consciousness of words has informed much of her growth. After she has united with her mother while they sing their duet, she thinks, "*Last night, the song was word up. Truth*" (91). And from that point on, Buhlaire uses "Word" as an interjection to indicate that she is speaking or thinking the truth (168, 173, 191). Buhlaire is aware of language as a shaping force of her subjectivity: until she knows the words of her father's and her mother's stories, she cannot know her self.

Having helped her father after she learns his story and then choosing to distance herself from him, Buhlaire returns to her matriarchal home better able to strengthen her relationship with her mother. Buhlaire communicates to Bluezy about wanting her to be home more often, and Buhlaire approves of her mother's romance with her Uncle Sam. Bluezy admits she has learned something from her daughter (162), and Buhlaire learns to accept her mother's career.

In the final chapter, Plain City floods in a January thaw, and Buhlaire helps her Uncle Sam pilot a rescue boat to evacuate various people, including her father, to safety. Buhlaire enjoys the flood, for it marks a change of the landscape as complete as what has occurred in her life: "It was funny. Everything was like it was over. Everything had changed, too. But not for the bad. *It's exciting, life is*" (191). She thinks of the boat as a metaphor for her own life: "*You sit in the boat, and it goes, and the motor goes. You forget it can't go by itself. It just looks like it does. There has to be somebody there to drive it*" (192). And in the final paragraph, her uncle does, in fact, "let her steer the boat home" (194). Buhlaire, "outside child" and proud of it, has claimed her own subject position.

MATERNAL NARRATIVE STRUCTURES

Some feminist novels rely on narrative structure as well as on content to communicate about relationships between mothers and daughters. A common pattern among feminist children's novels is the use of the "nested narrative," that is, of a plot structure in which a framing tale contains some sort of story-within-the-story.[6] The embedded narrative usually parallels the framing tale in both plot and theme. Gayle Greene comments on the prominence of embedded narratives as a mode of feminine communication when she describes their recurrence within postmodern feminist writing.[7] Greene defines the reason for the proliferation of the structure within recent women's novels as being a way for women to work through problems by revisiting them at different points in time in a pattern "which allows repetition with revision" (14). Greene notes that feminist critics and novelists alike have rejected the "linear sequence of traditional quests and *Bildungsroman* plots" in favor of more circular narratives; she cites Elizabeth Abel, Hélène Cixous, Julia Kristeva, and Patricia Tobin, among others, to demonstrate how this rejection of linear narrative form constitutes a rejection of patriarchal power structures (14–15). Thus, feminist children's novels with embedded narrative structures are potentially a source of social criticism.

Moreover, as is the case with many parallel embedded narratives written for adults, such texts written for children tend to emphasize discussions of art and of creativity because the story-within-a-story creates an atmosphere wherein the very nature of narrative becomes a fundamental issue. Embedded narratives therefore complicate sequential narrative linearity by demonstrating that "life, as well as novels, is constructed through frames, and that it is finally impossible to know where one frame ends and another begins" (Waugh, *Metafictions* 29). This self-reflexivity about the constructed nature of narratives implicitly lends itself to a critique of the dominant traditions of fictional realism (Waugh, *Metafictions* 28–34, 78).[8]

E. L. Konigsburg's *From the Mixed-Up Files of Mrs. Basil E. Frankweiler* (1967), Virginia Hamilton's *Arilla Sun Down*, and Paul Fleischman's *The Borning Room* (1991) all rely on narrative structure to explore either metaphorical or actual mother/daughter relationships. In the process, these books develop themes of birth and/or maternity to enact a positive reproduction of mothering. Part of how these children's novels use embedded narratives to communicate about maternity is the way they reproduce mothering not only thematically, by exploring maternal relationships and images, but also in the way that the texts reproduce mothering through narrative structure. In and of itself, the narrative structure of the embedded narrative evokes for the reader a textual representation of a mother's pregnant body. With its housing of one narrative body within another narrative, the structure implies feminine fertility, so nested narratives can themselves become a child-of-the-mother image; the subnarratives are the offspring of the narrative. The very structure of a nested narrative places a metaphorical value on birth.

Moreover, the maternal embedded narrative evokes the awareness of interpersonal connections that Gilligan associates with feminine decision making. The story-within-the-story establishes a weblike structure from within which a storyteller communicates about the importance of community. The structural pattern of the nested narrative represents the interconnectedness of narratives, while the thematic content of the story emphasizes the interconnectedness of relationships, especially between mother and daughter figures. Nested narratives that follow this pattern reproduce mothering in that they articulate the maternal process as a creative, artistic process. When this articulation occurs, the text joins form and function to glorify the maternal body. And this pattern may encourage child readers to question such social traditions as delegitimizing motherhood and such prescribed narrative traditions in children's literature as the linear plot.[9]

The relationship between artistic creation and procreation in *The Mixed-Up Files of Mrs. Basil E. Frankweiler* demonstrates how storytelling can be a means of achieving both subject formation and matrilineal community. Framed by the tale of Mrs. Frankweiler's relationship with her lawyer Saxonberg, the embedded narrative of *The Mixed-Up Files* contains the story of Claudia and her brother Jamie, who have run away to live in the Metropolitan Museum of Art. *The Mixed-Up Files* opens with the text's self-conscious prologue as Mrs. Frankweiler, the narrator, addresses her created reader, the lawyer Saxonberg. The text rhetorically asks this created reader, "*You never knew that I could write this well, did you?*" (3). The question asks the reader to acknowledge narrative creation; furthermore, the reader has been instructed to pay attention to the writing style. Storytelling affects the children's subject positions when Claudia and Jamie finally leave the museum and journey to see Mrs. Frankweiler. She values their secret, the story of their journey, enough to trade it for her secret about the origins of the Michelangelo sculpture. Once the children barter their story, it becomes a commodity. This transformation of their story into an object of exchange gives narrativity a specific value: narration gives the storyteller social power. Claudia and Jamie have the power to get what they want because they have a story to tell. And Claudia perceives herself differently once she learns from Mrs. Frankweiler the story behind Michelangelo's sculpture of the angel. Knowing Mrs. Frankweiler's story about the work of art changes Claudia's self-image, so a story has changed the girl's subject position.

After Claudia and Jamie share their stories with Mrs. Frankweiler and she shares the secret of the Michelangelo sculpture with them, the elderly woman expresses another secret: she feels wistful that she has never been a mother. She tells them, "Right now, I'd like to know how your mother feels" (154). Mrs. Frankweiler has concluded that having experienced the maternal subject position might have mattered more than the many works of art she possesses. In response to this assessment, the children make up their own fiction: they will adopt her as their grandmother. But they decide to keep their fiction a secret; they will not even tell Mrs. Frankweiler that she has given birth to foster grandchildren. In a sense, then, Claudia gives birth to her own grandmother while the older woman simultaneously experiences a vicarious maternity. In the end, Claudia and Mrs. Frankweiler share a maternal relationship that resides in the shared secrets of each other's narratives. And this maternal relationship has given them both strength.

Maternal relationships also carry great power in Virginia Hamilton's *Arilla Sun Down*. Storytelling gives the narrative persona of the text, the twelve-year-old Arilla, a sense of personal power. Arilla is trying to understand her own subject position as she works through her conflicted relationships with her mother, an African American dance teacher; her father, a Native American; and her brother, a teenager who rejects his African American heritage to embrace only his Native American heritage. Arilla admires her mother, but the girl mourns because she is not more like her. Arilla explains why she is not a dancer: "It'd be awful for [Mom] to have me so short and stubby next to her. I'd just be an embarrassment, and I'll never be tall, even if my legs are long" (26). Arilla also rejects her father and brother's identity; she is unable to remember that she did accept her Native American identity as a young child. A nested narrative structure emerges, then, because three embedded narratives describe those events about Arilla's connection with her tribal heritage that she does not consciously remember. In the opening of *Arilla Sun Down*, the elderly storyteller who is Arilla's friend tells the five year old: "*One day you will keep my stories . . . and you will truly be the name I have given you* [Wordkeeper]" (6). The reader thus knows from the start to pay attention to Arilla's story keeping.

The most important memory that Arilla has lost provides one key to her identity: she does not remember the friendship she has had as a young child with James Talking Story, a Native American who has named the young girl Wordkeeper, and with his wife, Susanne Shy Woman. Her partial amnesia has separated her from the powers that make her the Wordkeeper (20, 135−36, 235−36). But the framed tales about what Arilla has forgotten from her early childhood emphasize how storytelling affects an individual's subject position. Not only do the two narrative levels enable the reader to experience the completely different subject positions of Arilla as a five year old and Arilla as a twelve year old, but the embedded narratives also directly affirm storytelling as a function of subjectivity.[10]

In one of the embedded tales, Susanne Shy Woman describes the function of narrative as "telling stories about all of us, so we know one another, so we will come together as one" (92). Since this definition of story places direct value on interrelationships, the woman is instructing the girl to perpetuate what Carol Gilligan would see as the traditional role of woman as the protector of human attachment (23). According to Shy Woman, narratives are a way the subject can connect to other people, so stories are a way to form community. Moreover, Arilla participates in a maternal relationship with Shy Woman as the girl learns this message about community. Twice, the five year old refers to Susanne's maternity, calling her "Mother" and "Mama" (94, 95). And Shy Woman takes an active voice in disparaging social structures that have been determined by men. She comments, "No woman ever sign a treaty I know of, and maybe that's the reason a treaty never hold together" (91).

As a five year old, Arilla actually hears the creation of narratives expressed as a matter of maternity. The text links storytelling and procreation in the embedded narrative in which James Talking Story dies. After the storyteller's death, Arilla's father tells her that "it was a young woman who talked stories to the tribe and make [sic] the first chiefs" (168). The image implies that fertility is both physical and artistic; chiefs gain their power not only from being born of women but also from the narratives of women. Arilla's father goes on to tell her that "maybe you will be the one to talk stories again."

> "And so saying, making chiefs again?" [Arilla asks.]
> ". . . Maybe only to save the words in a memory pouch. Now and then, take out the words and cause us to be strong and not afraid." (169)

Arilla's father stresses the primacy of narrativity; in his extended metaphor, narrative is a maternal life force in and of itself. And since James Talking Story is also a story maker, the text clearly communicates that both males and females can engage in this form of social nurturance.

In the primary narrative, Arilla expresses regret that she does not have a little brother to nurture (109), but after she saves her older brother's life when he has fallen in an equestrian accident, the tension between them at least stabilizes. After that, Arilla feels she can begin to accept her brother, so she also begins to accept the portion of her heritage that is Native American. And as she does, her storytelling powers increase. She concludes her narrative thinking that maybe she will tell a story about her brother with some of the details changed to suit her style: "Maybe this is writing, changing things around and disguising the for-real" (247).

Arilla has come to realize that with storytelling she has the ability to shift not only her own subject position but her perception of other people's subjectivity. She expresses this recognition by describing ways she could tell stories about her mother. Arilla thinks, "I could write Mom on a horse just like I could write her as a dancer, or even on skates" (248). That Arilla has chosen to fictionalize her mother indicates that the girl finally accepts the differences between herself and her mother. And at least part of this acceptance resides in Arilla's self-recognition of herself as a teller of tales.

When the girl identifies herself once again as a storyteller at the end of the novel, she decides to rename herself, but not in terms of her brother—Arilla Sun Down—or in terms bestowed upon her by the tribal storyteller—Wordkeeper (248). Undecided about what exactly she will name herself, she says, "I could have a name for myself more than Sun Down. It'd be what I gave myself for what I do that's all my own. I sure will have to think about it" (248). Arilla knows that hereafter her subjectivity will be defined not as her mother's is, by dancing, but by writing. Storytelling has helped Arilla achieve individuation by providing her with a way to fit into her dual communities.

Paul Fleischman's *The Borning Room* is also informed by an embedded narrative structure. A woman named Georgina describes herself in the opening frame of the text. She tells the story of her birth in the first chapter of *The Borning Room* because she admits enjoying having heard the tale herself: "Two dozen times, two thousand times, Mama told this story—for the reason that I asked for it that often" (6). Georgina's subjectivity is indelibly embedded within this narrative. She reminisces to an initially unidentified listener about her life on the Ohio farm where she has lived for sixty-seven years. Much of her story focuses on the activities that have occurred in the borning room: her own birth; her helping her mother during the delivery of her brother Zeb; her grandfather's death; her mother's death while she delivers another son; Zeb's bout with whooping cough; and the birth of her own daughter, Emmaline. A central thread uniting these episodes is Georgina's love for her mother and her grief after her death, for Emmaline has been a loving and gentle mother.

The woman's death is clearly linked to the point Georgina is trying to make about life and death throughout her narration. Repeated throughout the story is imagery about the life cycle and the interconnectedness of all life. For instance, Georgina's grandfather once shook hands with Benjamin Franklin, so after she shakes hands with her newborn daughter, Georgina tells the baby "that she'd now shaken it too" (97). Georgina's stories about these cycles are part of the cycle itself; they are at once within and without the narrating of her life.

In the final framing chapter, the reader learns that Georgina is herself now lying waiting for death in the borning room. She seems not at all sad, for she understands that her birth and her death are all part of the nature of things. But the framing tale surrounding the book is itself a metaphor for her own life: in the opening frame she tells the story of her birth, and in the closing frame, the story of her death. Her narrative is her life. Furthermore, her discourse about her mother's maternity and her own maternity have situated her identity: she claims the maternal subject position for herself with pride. Even though it is written by a male author, *The Borning Room* sanctions maternity with the same metaphors and structure apparent in the novels by Konigsburg and Hamilton.

It seems no accident that the daughter figures in these nested narratives are girls who are either twelve years old or close to it. In *The Mixed-Up Files*, Claudia is one month shy of being twelve; Arilla turns twelve in the beginning of the framing tale of *Arilla Sun Down*. One of the stories that Georgina tells about herself occurs the summer she is twelve; it is the story of how she has learned from her grandfather's stories that all living things are spiritual. That these girls learn about the power of narrativity while they are on the brink of physical fertility creates a textual conjoining of artistry and maternity. As their bodies become capable of housing new life, their narratives become capable of housing new stories.

Moreover, those characters who have temporarily rejected their mothers (Claudia and Arilla) eventually return home either literally or metaphorically, if not to enmesh with their mothers, at least in acts that are symbolic acceptances of their mothers. This ability to accept their mothers' and their own subjectivities has been the result of matriarchal story sharing. While the girls in these novels work toward achieving individuation, they either listen to or they tell an empowering story. Claudia, Arilla, and Georgina all articulate their agency by participating in a narrative process that is evocative of and imbued with maternity. As a result of this process, all of them are better able to partake more fully in the mother/daughter relationship.

I would also like to mention briefly that *Walk Two Moons*, Sharon Creech's Newbery-winning novel, contains two embedded narratives that develop the pro/creation theme. The Native American narrator, Salamanca Tree Hiddle, is older than the protagonists of the other nesting narratives I have discussed in this section, and the text does not call the reader's attention to artistic creation as a construct as self-consciously. Still, *Walk Two Moons* affirms mothers' lives as independent from their children more than any text I have discussed in this chapter. As Salamanca drives with her grandparents from Ohio to her mother's grave in Idaho, she tells them the story of how her friend Phoebe's mother has grown assertive enough to include her first child, the son she had given up for adoption eighteen years earlier, in their family. As Phoebe begins to accept her mother's right to a life of her own, Salamanca begins to respect her mother's decision to leave their family after her second daughter died at birth. Salamanca's transcendence occurs when, through her storytelling, she finally reconciles herself to her mother's death by learning to appreciate her mother's individual humanity.

Such pro/creative nested narratives privilege maternal bonds when they communicate about the completeness of motherhood. Being a mother in these books is neither all good nor all bad, so they overcome the dualistic typology of mothering that concerns Chodorow (173–90) and that Daly and Reddy identify as culturally damaging (14). For example, both Claudia's mother in *The Mixed-Up Files* and Arilla's mother in *Arilla Sun Down* make mistakes. But these mothers' mistakes are not irredeemable; instead, they cast the mother as a fallible human who is neither perfect nor evil. These texts thus normalize motherhood. Within these narratives, maternity is simply part of the life process, albeit a necessary and beautiful part of it.

In overcoming their conflicts with their mothers through narrative acts imbued with maternity, the daughters gain some acceptance of maternity. Claudia accepts a surrogate mother; Arilla accepts her own and a surrogate mother; Georgina and Salamanca accept both their own mothers and themselves as maternal. The ideological implication critiques the traditional mythos that the mother exists only as an object of her children's subject formation (Hirsch, *Mother/Daughter Plot* 12). The women authors of these novels therefore overcome what Adrienne Rich cites as "matrophobia": "the fear not of one's mother or of motherhood but of *becoming one's mother*" (*Of Woman Born* 235). In these novels, maternity is liberating rather than restricting, empowering and creative rather than destructive. Inherent in this valuing of maternity is an ideological critique of society's tendency and, indeed, some feminists' tendency to delegitimize motherhood as an institution. With both the embedded narrative structure that evokes maternity and thematic content that consciously emphasizes maternity, these texts criticize denigrations of maternity.

The nested narrative in children's literature serves as a specifically feminist narrative that affirms one dimension of feminine power:

pro/creativity. In deviating from linear narrative structures, these texts provide an alternative structure that tends to be self-consciously critical of traditional story lines in children's literature. In employing birth imagery that parallels this alternative narrative structure, such texts also provide a positive interpretation of maternity. And in focusing on mother/daughter relationships, these novels define maternal relationships between women as a way for women and girls to support and to empower one another.

Although the daughter's story has been told throughout the history of children's novels, the mother's story has rarely been anything more than some sort of moral prescriptive. But the mothers' or mother figures' stories in *The Year It Rained, Prairie Songs, Plain City, The Mixed-Up Files of Mrs. Basil E. Frankweiler, Arilla Sun Down, The Borning Room,* and *Walk Two Moons* have complemented daughters' stories to communicate that feminine experience has a richness and a diversity that can only be understood if we look at its myriad expressions. Adrienne Rich writes about the diversity of female subject positions and how Western culture has repressed women-as-mothers by institutionalizing motherhood: "The culture makes it clear that neither the black mother, nor the white mother, nor any of the other mothers, are 'worthy' of our profoundest love and loyalty. Women are made taboo to women—not just sexually, but as comrades, cocreators, coinspiritors. In breaking this taboo, we are reuniting with our mothers; in reuniting with our mothers, we are breaking this taboo" (*Of Woman Born* 255). When feminist children's novelists create positive mother figures, they are subverting the restrictive traditions that Rich describes. Most specifically, they are rejecting the crippling Freudian masterplot that requires mothers and daughters to destroy each other at least psychically, if not literally. In creating mothers and mother figures like Mrs. Frankweiler and Bluezy who are "comrades, cocreators, coinspiritors" of their literal or metaphorical daughters, novelists such as Konigsburg and Hamilton revise the Freudian masterplot by maintaining that the mother/daughter relationship is more empowering than destructive.

Describing the early days of twentieth-century feminism, Rich writes:

It was not enough to *understand* our mothers; more than ever, in the effort to touch our own strength as women, we *needed* them. The cry of that female child in us need not be shameful or regressive; it is the germ of our desire to create a world in which strong mothers and strong daughters will be a matter of course.

We need to understand this double vision or we shall never understand ourselves. (225)

Carolyn Heilbrun echoes Rich's words when she theorizes that women have not only been traditionally silenced by the patriarchy but that we have also lacked our own stories to tell because we have served as objects in male plots ("Silence and Women's Voices" 4–5). Heilbrun proposes that women learn to tell new stories by connecting with the experiences of other women: "Our new fictions must come from our friendships, from the narratives we discover in encouraging each other and sharing our lives" ("Silence and Women's Voices" 10). Marianne Hirsch suggests that the narratives women share should specifically include those of motherhood when she states that in order "to demystify and politicize motherhood, and by extension female power more generally . . . , feminism might begin by listening to the stories that mothers have to tell, and by creating the space in which mothers might articulate those stories" (167).[11] As I noted earlier in this chapter, Barbara Johnson calls for much the same thing (143). Thus, when mothers tell their stories to their daughters, or to their sons and daughters, as Carrie does in Nina Bawden's *Carrie's War* (1973), they claim a position for maternity as a positive social institution.

Certainly, mothers' stories are a vital part of this empowering female interconnection that Rich, Heilbrun, Hirsch, and Johnson advocate. Female/female relationships are essential to feminist children's literature. And it is precisely in having developed the long-silenced voice of the mother that feminism has most influenced the dynamics of female interrelationships in children's novels.

8. METAFICTION AND THE POLITICS OF IDENTITY: NARRATIVITY, SUBJECTIVITY, AND COMMUNITY

That so many mothers have stories to tell in feminist children's novels calls our attention to the general tendency of the genre to be metafictional about storytelling. Metafictional writing, fiction about fiction itself, "self-consciously and systematically draws attention to its status as an artefact in order to pose questions about the relationship between fiction and reality" (Waugh, *Metafictions* 2). Anita Moss defines meta-fictional writing in children's literature as "works in which the imag-ined process by which the story is created becomes a central focus of the book" ("Varieties" 79).[1] Moss describes one use of metafiction as a way for an author to portray child writers in the "process of dis-covering their identities" (91). Moss subscribes to a fairly conventional definition of "identity" as something singular, fixed, and internally defined that a character can discover about herself; nevertheless, her point also applies to issues of subjectivity, for metafictional stories often depict children learning that their "identity" is actually so fluidly constructed by language that they hold a variety of subject positions. The self-consciousness of the metafictional language in the text, then, often underscores the child's growing consciousness of her own reliance on language. As a result, metafictional novels provide a culminating point for many of the issues I have discussed so far: language, storytellers and artist figures, voice, subjectivity, and community.

Elsewhere, I have argued that metafiction empowers the child reader by creating a place for her to enter the text and to solve some of the questions that metafictional passages often raise (Trites, "Is Flying Extraordinary?"). While the metafictional elements in such picture books as David Macaulay's *Black and White* (1990), Maira Kalman's *Max* books (e.g., *Max Makes a Million*, 1990), and Jon Scieszka and Lane Smith's books—notably *The Stinky Cheese Man* (1993)—are blatant efforts to call children's attention to books as constructs and the consequent construction of the reader as a subject, the metafiction in children's novels is often more subtle, and it is usually interwoven with embedded narratives and with questions about narrativity and language.

Narratives, obviously, are constructed by language. They have no other means of operating than through the principles of some language system. But if we accept the postmodern theories that define humans as constructed by language, as situated entirely within the principles of language systems, we notice that subjects are then like narratives, language-driven. Parallels between the two are not that hard to find in children's literature: authors often use a character's completion of an embedded narrative as a metaphor for the character's recognition of her agency. Harriet the Spy, for example, finishes the narrative she writes about Harrison Withers and sends it to the *New Yorker* before she makes amends with the classmates who have been ostracizing her. The completion of this narrative serves as a metaphor for both Harriet's growth and her sense of self-definition because language is so central to her understanding of her subjectivity. The text of *Harriet the Spy* demonstrates that language is communal and therefore dialogic: the growth that is the result of Harriet's recognizing the primacy of language occurs almost entirely as the result of her engaging in dialogues with other people.

Metafictional passages within a novel that call attention to the construction of narrative play an important role in affirming the dialogic nature of narratives. Feminist metafiction often asks the reader to think about the creation of narrative as something that occurs within a community, for the subject manipulating language to create a story usually does so for an audience (i.e., within a dialogue). While engaged with the linguistic process of story creation, the storyteller becomes aware of her subjectivity as a function of the language that necessarily occurs within a community. And her understanding of the social implications of the subject positions she holds is subsequently changed. A crucial stage in her growth, then, is recognizing that subjects exist within communities and that any subject position within a community is politically charged. Thus, as the character acknowledges her agency, she also becomes aware that her agency has an effect on other people. Because she affects them, they will have opinions of her, perceptions of her, that in turn affect her subjectivity.

Being aware that one's subjectivity has social implications leads the subject to recognize what I call the "politics of identity." I have noticed that few texts explore the issue as thoroughly as feminist metafictions do. For instance, before the protagonists in Virginia Hamilton's *Zeely* (1967), Avi's *The True Confessions of Charlotte Doyle* (1990), and Ursula K. Le Guin's *Tehanu* (1990) come to understand how their subjectivities are defined by narrative, they are confused and unable to participate fully in any community, but afterward, as they come to recognize the political implications of being constructed by language, they understand the intertwinings of narrativity, subjectivity, and community as residing within the politics of identity. They know that their subject positions, fluid as they are, are implicated in the politics of gender, race, class, culture, religion, family, and innumerable other social institutions. Their growing awareness is the direct result of storytelling that creates a number of metafictional passages.

Take, for example, Virginia Hamilton's *Zeely*. The protagonist, Elizabeth, occupies not one but at least three of the marginalized subject positions that Cassie Logan occupies in Mildred Taylor's novels: Elizabeth is a child, she is female, and she is black. Narrative takes on tremendous importance for this character as she learns that her sense of herself need not be shaped by racist or sexist notions of what it means to be an African American girl. She learns this lesson within a dialogical experience of storytelling that she shares with another female. The story begins as Elizabeth and her brother journey to visit their uncle on his farm. She says, "I ought to make up something special just because we've never ever gone alone like this" (7).

When the train they are riding emerges from a tunnel, signifying a metaphorical (re)birth, the girl decides what the "special thing" will be: she will rename herself and her brother. She decides that she will be "Geeder" and he will be "Toeboy" for the rest of the summer (9). "Geeder" reflects the girl's desire to be able to call mares to her at the farm, and "Toeboy" reflects her brother's desire to walk bare-footed all summer. Both nicknames indicate that the children yearn for freedom to explore their agency, but Geeder's desire is also specifically articulated as a wish to call *female* horses to her; it is a clear wish to connect with femininity. Moreover, the children's new sense of their own identities reside entirely in words. The children have not changed, only the words describing them have, but those words have the power to change each child's self-image and thus each of their subject positions. The renaming establishes the most important creative power that Geeder will display throughout the book: she invents stories to experiment with the creative power of her own subjectivity.

The most prominent story that Geeder invents involves her under-standing of a local farm woman. When Geeder first sees Zeely Tayber, a six-and-a-half-foot-tall descendant of the African Watsusi tribe, the girl becomes infatuated with the woman. Zeely is a silent and with-drawn woman who communicates better with the hogs she farms than she does with anyone else, even her father. Zeely's relationship with her father demarcates the gender politics that inform the book: when the two are driving their hogs to market, Zeely coaxes the balk-ing animals along with food while her father beats them with long poles. The difference between their gender-based attitudes toward the animals is almost stereotypical. But eventually, Zeely stands up to her bullying father: "Zeely grabbed Nat's wrist. The pole stood poised and trembling in the air and mist. Zeely looked long and hard at Nat. Her lips moved as she spoke softly to him. Nat twisted the pole. It jerked toward Zeely's head and then, slowly, came down to rest at Nat's side" (73). With her words and with her gentleness, Zeely has rendered Nat and his brutality at least symbolically impotent. There is no doubt that the text values Zeely's feminine methods over Nat's masculine ones. In this instance, Hamilton relies on stereotypes about men and women in the type of feminist stance that praises femininity and condemns masculinity that I discuss in chapter 6.

Nevertheless, after seeing Zeely with the hogs, Geeder explains Zeely's stateliness to herself when she sees a magazine picture of a Watsusi queen who looks much like Zeely. Because of the similarity, Geeder decides Zeely *is* a queen. In a metafictional process that demonstrates how central language is to the girl's understanding of herself, Geeder spins tales about Zeely. All her daydreams involve communicating with and connecting with another female; in one, she and Zeely talk to each other, and in another, Zeely is a queen and Geeder is the only person who is allowed to talk to her (36, 52). Geeder intuitively knows that words are the key to her place in any community.

After she discovers the picture, Geeder reaches out for the first time to play with the other children in the local community. The form of play in which she engages is to establish a public persona as a storyteller in order to convince them that Zeely is royal. Geeder's dialogic interactions with the other children revolve entirely around the process of creating fiction. But one of the boys who listens to Geeder's storytelling interrupts to tell her that a Watsusi heritage is nothing to value, for the Watsusis have enslaved other people (56). Geeder denies this voice of rationality, telling the boy that Zeely is "still a queen" (56). He then pronounces her a "silly girl" (58), and Geeder leaves, severing her short-lived interaction with other children. Her self-created and self-creating fictions are more important to her than either cold, rational facts or the people who believe them. Her subject position as story creator is, for now, more satisfying than any other position she can perceive for herself to take in a community.

When Zeely discovers that Geeder has been spreading this narrative throughout the community, Zeely asks to meet with the girl. They do, in a dark glade of the forest, and Zeely explains that she understands Geeder's efforts to grapple with identity issues. Zeely tells Geeder, "You are very much the way I was at your age," which pleases the girl. Zeely goes on to explain: "I mean that because you found this picture, you were able to make up a good story about me. I once made up a story about myself, too" (95). Zeely then talks about how she pretended to be a Watsusi queen when she was a girl. The pretense was the only way she knew how to explain to herself why she was so different from the other children around her: why she was so much taller (and although the text never explicitly explains it, since she was living in Canada as a child, perhaps why she was so much darker-skinned than many of the other Canadian children). At the time, this narrative gave Zeely a sense of herself; fictions of her own making gave her power.

Zeely then tells Geeder two tales that underscore the importance of accepting one's subject positions with pride. Disappointed that Zeely refuses to define herself as a queen, Geeder tells Zeely that she wants to be different, the way Zeely is. Geeder desires to occupy a different subject position. And the woman understands. She knows the girl wants to be "whoever it is you are when you're not being Geeder. . . . The person you are when you're not making up stories. Not Geeder and not even me, but yourself—is that what you want, Elizabeth? . . . I stopped making up tales a long time ago . . . and now I am myself" (114). In conclusion, Zeely tells Geeder, "You have a most fine way of dreaming. . . . Hold on to that" (115). And although Geeder is startled by Zeely's perceptiveness, she is also pleased. The girl has not gained the type of connection with Zeely that she had hoped for because Zeely will never be her exclusive property, but Geeder does have a memory now that will help her to understand the difference between narratives that help and narratives that harm.

Even more important, Geeder is willing to interact with other people after she has established a connection with Zeely. Throughout the novel she has prized her solitude, pushing her brother away and having little to do with anyone else. But once she has established the type of human contact she has wanted, she turns to her family, ready once again to be a part of the community. This reconnection with the community is only made possible by the words of a woman's narratives that validate the girl's sense of self. Metafictionally affirming her subject position as a storyteller, Geeder tells Zeely's stories to her brother and uncle. When she is finished, she proclaims to them that Zeely is still a queen of "the best kind" because she manages to retain her dignity even though she lives in sordid conditions with a brutal father. To affix Zeely in her memory, Geeder names a star in the woman's honor, providing yet another example of her naming something to claim it for herself. Geeder is still a storyteller, but perhaps one who sees herself more clearly because she has had the chance to connect with a female mentor. The mentor has taught Geeder to value the words that define her and to use them wisely so that she can take pride in her heritage and in her place within the community.

Written more than twenty years after *Zeely*, Avi's *The True Confessions of Charlotte Doyle* is both more self-consciously metafictional and more self-consciously feminist than Hamilton's novel is. *The True Confessions of Charlotte Doyle* contains a variety of statements that call the reader's attention to the construction of narrative as a tool of community building. Narrated in the first person, the story opens with Charlotte's metafictional statement at the end of the first sentence that "my story is worth relating even if it did happen years ago" (1). Her story is the tale of how she, the daughter of a New England ship owner, sailed aboard a trading ship in 1832. When the ship sets sail, Charlotte has no female chaperon aboard because of an unfortunate series of accidents. This lack of chaperonage leads her to be self-conscious of her status as Other: she is all too aware of being the only female in a male world. She is also an insufferable snob and a slave to the Cult of True Womanhood at the story's opening. Much of the tale involves Charlotte's growing recognition of the folly of her classism, racism, and sexism, which makes the book as politically correct, if perhaps occasionally historically incorrect, as it could be. But the political correctness emphasizes how other people's perceptions of anyone's subject positions can have radical sociopolitical implications for everyone involved.

The story of how Charlotte switches loyalty from the brutal, insane, and upper-class Captain Jaggery to the mutineering members of the crew is a gripping one. Charlotte overcomes her prejudices and the sense of Otherness that has been the result of her bigotry so well that she actually becomes a working member of the crew. After Jaggery falls from the ship while he has been trying to attack this "unnatural" girl, as he calls Charlotte, the members of the crew appoint Charlotte captain. In that sense, Avi's critique of classism is easily deconstructed because the status quo is restored; the only non-working-class person left alive on the ship is the only one the crew is comfortable appointing captain. Class codes, in this case, prove to have more power than gender codes. Remaining true to the codes of her class, one of Charlotte's first acts as captain is to record in the log that Captain Jaggery fell overboard during a hurricane so that he will be remembered as a hero rather than as a murderer. After this act of narrative reconstruction, Charlotte cynically and metafictionally remarks, "I have been skeptical of accounts of deceased heroes ever since" (196).

The text of *The Adventures of Charlotte Doyle* makes clear that Charlotte gains an understanding of her agency from the process of writing and of constructing her narrative. Early on she tells the reader that the journal her father has required her to keep during her sea voyage has made it possible for her to retell her tale: "Keeping that journal then is what enables me to relate now in perfect detail everything that transpired during that fateful voyage across the Atlantic Ocean in the summer of 1832" (3). Without having first written her story, Charlotte's self-understanding would be incomplete. The journal does not gain its full significance, however, until Charlotte returns to her home in Providence. While still on the ship, Charlotte imagines herself telling her tale to her family. "With great vividness I pictured myself relating my adventure, while they, grouped about, listened in rapt, adoring attention, astonished yet proud of me. At the mere anticipation, my heart swelled with pride" (181). Her image of narrative construction at this point is that it can build community by helping her interact with her family; she thinks her narratives can help her to assume a subject position of strength with them. With this fantasy inspiring her, she carefully records all the events of the mutiny that led to her joining the crew and to Jaggery's death in her journal. "I wrote furiously in my journal, wishing to set down everything. It was as if only by reliving the events in my own words could I believe what had happened" (196).

But when Charlotte returns to Providence and begins to tell the tale to her family, her father silences her, not wanting to hear that his daughter has unsexed and declassed herself. Moreover, Mr. Doyle is angered that Charlotte's journal does not contain the "sober account" he has sought (200); instead, it contains a truth that he does not want to hear. To silence her, and to deny the truth that so angers him, Mr. Doyle burns Charlotte's journal, explaining:

I have read your journal carefully. I have read some of it—*not all*— to your mother. I could say any number of things, but in fact will say only a few. When I have done we shall *not* speak of any of this again. . . . What you have written is rubbish of the worst taste. Stuff for penny dreadfuls! Beneath contempt. Justice, Charlotte, is poorly served when you speak ill of your betters such as poor Captain Jaggery. More to the point, Charlotte, your spelling is an absolute disgrace. Never have I seen such abominations. And the grammar . . . it is beyond *belief*! (206–07)

Mr. Doyle attempts both to silence Charlotte and to repress her. His launching into grammar as a more important matter than the life-and-death adventures Charlotte has experienced puts into perfect clarity the man's understanding of her subject position: he thinks it should be an object position. Girls, in his opinion, should have neither a voice nor a sense of their own agency. But the text wants such an attitude to anger the reader. It certainly angers Charlotte, who chooses to run away, resuming her place as a crew member aboard the *Seahawk*.

The novel ends with Charlotte repudiating her birth family and adopting the crew of the ship as her family; she tells them, "I've decided to come home" (210). In the final sentence of the book, her friend Zacariah tells her, "A sailor . . . chooses the wind that takes the ship from safe port . . . but winds have a mind of their own" (210). His words reflect Charlotte's understanding that she does have a certain amount of agency over her life but not complete control. What she can control, however, is the narrative she tells herself about who she is. And she can control to whom she tells that narrative. Thus, she picks the community aboard the *Seahawk* because they are willing to accept her agency as her family will not. She chooses to live where other people's perceptions of her subjectivity are not stifling; she chooses to live where being female does not force her to abdicate her agency. The writing process has been crucial throughout *The Adventures of Charlotte Doyle* in helping Charlotte come to better understand her own sense of her selfhood; as a result, metafiction in this novel is inextricably linked to the politics of her identity.

The fourth book of Ursula K. Le Guin's *Earthsea* series, *Tehanu*, was written as a corrective to the unconscious sexism in the first three novels of *Earthsea*, and in that sense it has an even clearer feminist agenda than does *The True Confessions of Charlotte Doyle*.[2]

Le Guin's entire fantasy series is based on the premise that names give objects and people their power; wizards are the most powerful people in the land because they can intuit the names of all things. Thus, all four of the *Earthsea* books emphasize the primacy of language. Words, especially names-as-words, exist as an integral part of an object's or person's subjectivity; nothing can be completely known or understood until its name is known as well.

In the first three of the *Earthsea* books, published between 1968 and 1972, only men have the power to know anything's true name. But in *Tehanu*, written two decades later, the old order dies away, and women are finally shown to have the same capacity. Len Hatfield identifies this ideological change as a revolution against "the patriarchal order that has dominated Earthsea until now" (58–59). Early in the story, Ogion, a powerful wizard, lies dying. Among his last words are an enigmatic entreaty to his ward, Tenar, to teach her ward, Therru, "all" (21). Ogion cryptically tells Tenar, "The dragon . . . Over . . . All changed!—Changed, Tenar!" (23). No one, the reader included, knows quite what Ogion means at the time, but as the story unfolds, the meaning of his prophetic words becomes clear. Ged, the protagonist of the first three *Earthsea* books and the archwizard of Earthsea, has lost his magical powers while fighting to repair a hole torn between the worlds of the living and the land of the dead. In *Tehanu*, a mighty dragon returns the disempowered Ged from his battle to the shores of his homeland, but the archwizard is too late to see Ogion's death. Nevertheless, Tenar nurses Ged back to physical if not spiritual health, and the reader slowly discerns that during the battle Ged fought, everything "changed," as Ogion predicted, so that those whose powers the male wizards have previously shunned—women and dragons—will be restored to power. As Len Hatfield notes, women and dragon both represent a patriarchal notion of Other in the first three *Earthsea* books (48), for only men define what is Other and what is not. This shared Otherness makes the politics of women's and dragons' identity quite similar.

Throughout the *Earthsea* trilogy, women's power is typified as either weak or evil; the phrases *"weak as woman's magic"* and *"wicked as woman's magic"* are repeated numerous times. But in *Tehanu* the phrases are for the first time repeated with irony as Tenar begins to question just why it is that women's magic should be so maligned.

Questioning the labels that the male-dominated society has placed on her, she asks a friend who is a witch, "What's wrong with men?" (51). The witch's answer is enmeshed in the politics of identity:

> I don't know my dearie. I've thought on it. . . . The best I can say it is like this. A man's in his skin, see, like a nut in its shell. . . . It's hard and strong, that shell, and it's all full of him. Full of grand man-meat, man-self. And that's all. That's all there is. It's all him and nothing else, inside. . . . a woman's a different thing entirely. Who knows where a woman begins and ends? Listen, mistress, I have roots, I have roots deeper than this island. Deeper than the sea, older than the raising of the lands. . . . no one knows, no one can say what I am, what a woman is, a woman of power, a woman's power, deeper than the roots of trees, deeper than the roots of islands, older than the Making, older than the moon. (51–52)

Perhaps no one dares say what women are, but the witch's answer makes clear that she thinks the difference between them and men is the difference between solipsism and community: a man is nothing but himself; a woman is everything, including roots tying her to other roots. According to this stereotypical and Gilliganesque ideological position, then, men are detached from and women attached to the people around them. Tenar even thinks of her love for Therru as an image straight out of Gilligan: "Love, her love for Therru and Therru's for her, made a bridge across that gap, a bridge of spider web" (*Tehanu* 155; Gilligan 32).

That the majority of men in Earthsea perceive women as inferior is clear. The most common way they subjugate women is by silencing them, as when an evil wizard deprives Tenar of language (123, 216–18) or when a good but unenlightened wizard ignores Tenar's wisdom and so does not respond to her during their conversation (144–45). Ged, the now-powerless archwizard, tells Tenar that a woman could never be archwizard because wizards' "power is the power of men, their knowledge is the knowledge of men. Both . . . are built on one rock: power belongs to men. If women had power, what would men be but women who can't bear children? And what would women be but men who can?" (197). According to Ged's definition, which does much to refute the essentializing definition of the difference between men and women that the witch has used, there really is no difference between them other than the ability to bear children, but the people of Earthsea have as yet to learn that lesson.

The text's debate about the politics of gender identity is reinforced by questions about the identity of the dragons. It is through them and through Tenar's ward, Therru, that metafiction and the politics of identity come together in this text. Therru is an eight-year-old girl, the child of vagrants; her father and his friends have beaten and raped her. With the complicity of the girl's mother, these men have left the unconscious child to burn to death in their campfire, but she miraculously survives. Tenar raises her, accepting the girl's scarred face and arm, for Therru is blind in one eye and has only a charred stump for a fist on the right side (33). Therru is obsessed with fire. She frequently describes red objects as "fire" (see, e.g., 16), and she is often burning hot to Tenar's touch (135). The name "Therru" even means "burning, the flaming of fire" (21).

Therru's favorite story is one that holds the key to who she is. Tenar tells her this story early in the text; it is about the time when dragons and humans were one. "They were all one people, one race, winged, and speaking the True Language. They were beautiful, and strong, and wise, and free" (11). But those dragons who were obsessed with "flight and wildness" remained dragons, while those who "gathered up treasure, wealth, things made, things learned" eventually became human (11). Those humans who cherished the original wisdom and knew the language of the dragons, however, became the wizards (12). According to the myth, certain people "still both human and dragon . . . live in peace, great winged beings both wild and wise, with human mind and dragon heart" (12). One final attribute of dragons has semiological implications: unlike humans, dragons are one with their language: "They do not learn. . . . They are" (196). After hearing this narrative, Therru falls in love with the concept of dragons; they obviously represent for her the agency she feels she does not have. And that agency is clearly linked to semiological power, the power words hold as signs.

Yet as the story progresses and the wizards of Earthsea search for a new archwizard to replace Ged, the reader begins to suspect that Therru might be closer to possessing the power of the dragons than she herself realizes. One wizard predicts that knowledge of the next archwizard will come from a woman (142), and the neighborhood witch refuses to take Therru as an apprentice because she is too powerful (163). In the final pages of the novel, Earthsea finds its new archwizard, and it is indeed Therru. But the surprise comes when her origins are revealed: the wisest and oldest of dragons, Kalessin, comes when Therru calls to it in the ancient language, the language of semiological unity.[3] Kalessin in turn calls her by her true name, "Tehanu," which is the name of a bright star, and the dragon identifies the girl as one of its children.[4] At last, Therru/Tehanu learns that she is one of the dragon people, but because of her love for Tenar and Ged, she chooses to stay and serve the humans with whom she also shares a culture. Kalessin, however, promises that in time it will return for her (222–23). The politics of Tehanu's identity has resided within a narrative all along; the pretty myth spun as a tale to amuse the child has held the key to the subject positions she occupies. The metafictional elements of narrative and language have combined to demonstrate the politics of her identity: the greatest wizard will be one who has both the strength of the dragon and the strength of a woman; the greatest wizard's subjectivity resides in the wisdom of ancient narratives. Without the language of those ancient narratives, Tehanu would have no power.

The metafictional passages in *Tehanu*, *Charlotte Doyle*, and *Zeely* all revolve around the politics of identity: what it means to be female, what it means to be Other, and what it means to refuse to be Other. And the metafiction is often subversive. *Zeely* uses a narrative to convince Geeder that belonging to an upper class like royalty is not the only way to avoid Otherness; Charlotte uses the writing of a narrative to affirm her subjectivity and to indict the male-dominated culture that refuses to accept it; Therru learns from a narrative that she, a child, has more power than anyone in her world because of the subject positions she alone can adopt. Metafictional passages in a number of other children's novels have similar implications: E. L. Konigsburg's *From the Mixed-Up Files of Mrs. Basil E. Frankweiler*; Hunter's *The Sound of Chariots*; Lawrence Yep's *Dragonwings* (1975); Virginia Hamilton's *Arilla Sun Down* and *The Magical Adventures of Pretty Pearl*; MacLachlan's *Arthur, for the First Time, Cassie Binegar, Unclaimed Treasures*, and *The Facts and Fictions of Minna Pratt*; Cleary's

Dear Mr. Henshaw; Voigt's *Jackaroo*; Pam Conrad's *My Daniel* (1989); Block's *Weetzie Bat* and its sequels; Paul Fleischman's *The Borning Room*, and Sharon Creech's *Walk Two Moons* all contain metafictional passages that link the construction of narrative to the construction of subjectivity.

That so many feminist children's novels contain metafictional passages has several implications. On the most basic level, these metafictions attest to the creation of story as a source of personal strength when the creation of story and the creation of self are connected; metafictions demonstrate narrative as a process of subject formation. More important, metafictions demonstrate the primacy of language. In all three of the cases I have discussed in this chapter, the language of narrative is a *cause* more than an *effect* of the character's subjectivity, so the character is, as Lacan would maintain, constructed by language, but the language occurs in a dialogic process that encourages the character (and therefore the reader) to think of herself in terms of the subject positions she holds within a community. Zeely and Geeder interact in their storytelling, as do Therru and Tenar. Charlotte's dialogue occurs more directly with the reader, but in all three novels, the process of narrative as a source of subject formation resides within the necessity of dialogics: the subject must have an audience, and when she does, she has a community through which or against which she can understand her subjectivity. Thus, metafiction can only occur within relationships: narratives must have both a teller and an audience. And so, too, do children learn to recognize their subjectivity; it exists as a constantly shifting construct of relationships.

I find it significant that these three novels represent different phases of feminism. *Zeely* has emerged from an early African American feminism that notes the inseparability of racial and gender issues for black women.[5] *Charlotte Doyle* reflects feminist revisionism and the efforts of feminists to rewrite and claim traditionally male narratives (in this case the archetypal mutiny narrative) for females. *Tehanu* speculates about the possibility of male and female power coexisting in harmony. Nevertheless, all three novels affirm femininity. I find it interesting as well that these novels cross genre lines. One is contemporary realism for early novel readers, one historical realism for middle school readers, and one high fantasy for young adult readers. Furthermore, their authors cross racial and gender boundaries: Hamilton is a black woman, Le Guin a white woman, and Avi a white man. But despite coming from different ideological positions and despite covering different generic categories, the novels all share a common implication: metafiction can serve as a way to communicate to readers that the politics of identity resides in community.

9. AFTERWORD:

FEMINIST PEDAGOGY AND

CHILDREN'S LITERATURE

Children's literature as a field of study has grown during the 1990s for a number of reasons. One is the burgeoning acceptance of all marginalized literatures within literary criticism as a whole; another is the push from the whole language movement, by whatever name it is called, to integrate children's and adolescent literary texts into elementary and secondary classrooms. Children's publishing, too, has become both more prolific and more sophisticated, providing critics with rich materials to analyze. I hope that in time these three industries will work even more closely together, for academic criticism and primary education are as surely industrialized as book publishing is. The profit motive might seem to be different, the goal may be more to generate knowledge than money, but all three function indisputably around some drive for profit. Since educators at all levels are invested in seeing their students succeed, teachers are as immersed in the economics of the marketplace as book publishers are, whether they want to admit it or not.

I see a shared profit, however, for all three industries in advancing feminist children's books. Books which empower girls to recognize and claim their subject positions empower the entire culture, for our society can only grow stronger as we teach our children to be

stronger. I am certainly not the first to say it—in fact, I'm echoing
Mary Wollstonecraft's two-hundred-year-old *Vindication of the Rights
of Woman* (1792)—but when we educate girls to feel equal to boys,
the entire society improves.

Much of the education necessary to that improvement has begun
in the college classrooms where future teachers are trained how to
teach children. But as a feminist pedagogue who teaches quite a
number of education majors, I often encounter resistance to my
classroom politics and my attempts to foster equality, especially in
the early parts of the semester. For too many of my students, feminism connotes stridency, male bashing, radical rejections of traditions they like, and claiming victim status. But during the course of
the semester, I encourage my students to think of feminism as existing in the positive as well as in the negative. For every stereotype I
show them, I try to demonstrate a stereotype being broken. After
every immersion in masculinist ideology, I offer them an immersion
in feminist ideology. Whenever we talk about how socialization creates gender-linked weaknesses, we also talk about gender-linked
and non-gender-specific strengths.

Nevertheless, tensions in my classroom usually erupt about the
time we begin talking about *The Little Mermaid*. I invariably want to
talk about Andersen's version; they prefer to talk about Disney's, so
we compromise and discuss both. One semester in particular, a class
rejected vehemently my assertion that Disney's version of the story is
even more sexist than Andersen's original story.[1] A student named
Ann led the defense against Disney; she maintained that Disney's little
mermaid, Ariel, is a strong female who pursues what she wants and
gets it. Ann was horrified that I thought there was something wrong
with Ariel's marrying Eric at the end because "that's so romantic
and the book is so sad." Ann particularly objected to my critique of
Disney's phallocentric and gynophobic imagery on two grounds:
"Surely," she said, "the Disney critics aren't doing it on purpose, and
besides, kids never notice stuff like that anyway." I could sense her
frustration with me, and because I remembered the frustration of
losing an almost identical argument in my undergraduate children's literature class at Texas A&M University in 1980 when I
stubbornly insisted that Disney's *Snow White* was as valid a version
of the story as the Grimms' because Disney's rendition reflects our

culture rather than nineteenth-century German culture, I tried to validate Ann's arguments. At the same time, however, I wanted to defend my own position: whether or not the artists are conscious of creating sexist images and whether or not children are aware of perceiving them, both groups are involved in perpetuating ancient symbols of female repression. I suggested to Ann that perhaps she couldn't see the sexism involved because she had been taught so carefully by a sexist culture that female repression was normal. She left class that day practically in tears, I later found out. My feminist pedagogy had failed, or perhaps I had failed it. I had used my power to silence a woman, which is exactly what I was accusing Disney of doing.

My story, however, has a happy ending that unfolded in two parts, both of which had more to do with Ann than with me. During the next class, Ann announced that she and a group of her friends had watched the movie after our last discussion and that she had been appalled to discover that perhaps I was right after all: she could see that many of the positive symbols of power in the movie were phallic and that many of the negative symbols were gynophobic. Even worse, one of her friends pointed out the very distinct penis drawn into the castle on the cover of the videotape. "They *do* know what they're doing," she said, referring to the Disney artists. "They're doing it on purpose!" And then she wanted to know the answer to a question I could not adequately answer: "Why are they doing that?" I thought it was too facile to say that the patriarchy wanted to perpetuate female repression and too naive to say that they were just reflecting the culture the way they had learned it. But Ann's conversion to feminism made my confusion worthwhile.

She took another class from me the following semester, and while we were studying Patricia MacLachlan's *Unclaimed Treasures*, she was one of the text's most vocal advocates. When several of her classmates wanted to dismiss it as "just a girl's book," she pressed the issue, wanting to know why that somehow made it a second-class novel in their eyes. She was excited that the protagonist had a strong voice, "even after she's married—unlike Ariel in *The Little Mermaid*," she told them. And when that group started defending Disney's mermaid, she invited them to watch the video with her so they "could see" what she was talking about. This story would just be another example of indoctrination—how I have successfully brainwashed someone to accept my ideology instead of someone else's, hooray for me and score one for our side—except for one thing. Ann used a different strategy to convince her classmates than I had used. She improved on my technique by offering them a community in which to learn and to voice their opinions; she wanted them to watch the video with her so that she could share her excitement with them more than she wanted to inflict her judgments on them. I learned something important from Ann that day.

Since then, I have been even more focused on the positive aspects of feminism: on the ways females interact, the ways females communicate, the ways females find their voices, the ways females have revised patriarchal images, and the ways females use fictional constructs to communicate their ideologies to the reader. My goal for this book has been to provide that type of reading of children's literature. I hope my ideas can inspire students at all levels of children's literature to think positively about feminism so that they can in turn as teachers, students, critics, publishers, writers, librarians, booksellers, and parents communicate about the completeness of humanity to children. I want everyone who enters a classroom with a children's book in her or his hand to recognize the politics of the text, regardless of the age of the students in the class. And I want every editor of children's books, every writer of children's books, every reader of children's books to be aware of the myriad possibilities of feminist expression. Far from being a limiting genre with a vision narrowed only to praising females at the expense of males, the feminist children's novel recognizes the potential of all people and proclaims that potential.

Too often college professors tell students that they can't change anything, that they need to accept the system if they want to be successful within it. I try to communicate the exact opposite to them. To me, success lies in changing an unsuccessful system. If most of my students validate only twenty-five children in their lives, but those twenty-five children grow up to influence twenty-five more children to be less sexist, we can, indeed, change the world in time. I know of no more powerful tool than children's books to use in the process, for books are readily available, and unlike most of the texts the entertainment industry churns out, innumerable books already exist that reject sexism. The materials for us to continue changing our culture are already at hand; now all we need to do is use those materials as fully as we can.

We can use feminist children's books in a number of already established areas. Certainly, every college-level children's literature course should include feminist children's novels. If we expose future teachers to the choice materials in the field, they will then be well-positioned to revise the standard reading lists in the public and private schools that contain the same tired, masculinist tracts that were worn out when I was in grade school: *Johnny Tremain*, *My Brother Sam Is Dead*, *Treasure Island*. This process of revision is already, of course, well under way, but it seems to me that teachers are still choosing masculinist texts like *Maniac Magee* and *The Whipping Boy* over feminist texts for fear of alienating male readers. The reasoning goes something like, "Well, the girls will read anyway, so we'd better pick books that will appeal to the boys." I maintain that we carefully teach boys to be alienated by female protagonists from the very first class in which we ask them to say how they "identify with the protagonist." As Perry Nodelman puts it, "In training children to identify, to read only about themselves, we sentence them to the solitude of their own consciousness" ("How Typical" 184). Why not ask them instead to think about how interesting or unique the characters are, how different they are from us, what we learn from them, how they change? Why not simply assume that it is as natural for a boy to read a book about a girl as it is for a girl to read a book about a boy? And why not provide students with books that show both girls and boys who are interesting, active, vocal, and powerful? To do any less is to cheat our students of half the world.

Teachers who provide children with feminist texts that balance the sexist classics many of us still feel compelled to teach are practicing feminist pedagogy. Teachers who use nonsexist multicultural texts are practicing feminist pedagogy. Teachers who validate female voices as clearly as they validate male voices in their classrooms are practicing feminist pedagogy. Teachers who allow their students to make self-empowering choices are practicing feminist pedagogy. Teachers who listen when their students voice dissenting opinions are practicing feminist pedagogy. Teachers who recognize how their students are socially constructed to occupy a number of oftentimes conflicting subject positions are practicing feminist pedagogy. Fortunately, since from its inception the study of children's literature has been dedicated to claiming the importance of an entirely disfranchised population, children's literature classrooms often lend themselves easily to such feminist practices. And so, too, does the literature itself.

Thus, I hope that *Waking Sleeping Beauty* provides people who work with children material to revise gender stereotypes and to replace them with more complete visions of females in children's books. Rethinking gender roles is an ongoing process, and the study here only comprises one small part of that process. But if I have participated in the debate, continued the process, provided new ways of thinking about the subject, then I have met my goal.

NOTES

· · · · · ·

PREFACE

1. Referring to "feminism" in the singular implies erroneously that what is actually a polymorphous and polyvocal set of theories, movements, and political actions has a unified number of principles. This is far from the case, but because referring to those sets of principles that advocate women's issues as "feminisms" is stylistically cumbersome, I will use the term "feminism" herein.

2. For some excellent commentaries on sexism in children's books, I refer the reader to works by the following authors cited in my bibliography: Ruth Bottigheimer, Bob Dixon, Mem Fox, Lois Rauch Gibson, Mary Ritchie Key, Carole M. Kortenhaus and Jack Demarest, Deborah Langerman, Alleen Pace Nilsen, P. Gila Reinstein, John W. Stewig and Mary L. Knipfel, Kay Vandergrift, J. Weitzman et al., and Sharon Wigutoff.

3. I refer the reader to scholarship listed in my bibliography by such scholars as Beverly Lyon Clark, Elizabeth Keyser, Lois Kuznets, Mitzi Myers, and Lissa Paul, for examples.

1. DEFINING THE FEMINIST CHILDREN'S NOVEL

1. For a succinct analysis of how ideology operates in children's books, see Peter Hollindale, "Ideology and the Children's Book."

2. Bob Dixon provides a historical survey of sexism in British and American literature in *Catching Them Young 1: Sex, Race, and Class in Children's Fiction*. He investigates the following manifestations of gender indoctrination: "physical movement and deportment; speech; role-enforcement and dress and, lastly, there's the reward for conformity, the gilt on the cage" in novels by Louisa May Alcott, Susan Coolidge, Noel Streatfield, and Grace Allen Hogarth (7). He devotes an entire chapter of the second volume, *Catching Them Young 2: Political Ideas in Children's Fiction*, to Enid Blyton's sexism.

2. SUBVERTING STEREOTYPES

1. Anna E. Altmann's "Welding Brass Tits on the Armor" analyzes

McKinley's use of archetypal patterns in *The Blue Sword*'s prequel, *The Hero and the Crown*, in detail.

2. Karen Cushman's *Catherine, Called Birdy* (1994) is an example of a text that violates historical integrity to present a feminist protagonist. Catherine is a marvelously articulate and independent character, but her actions, especially her literacy, seem unbelievable for a thirteenth-century girl.

3. SUBJECTIVITY AS A GENDER ISSUE

Portions of this chapter first appeared as an article, "Claiming the Treasures: Patricia MacLachlan's Organic Postmodernism," *Children's Literature Association Quarterly* 18 (1993): 23–28.

1. Although Lacan is a notorious misogynist, I follow feminist critics from Catherine Belsey to Juliet Flower MacCannell who find in Lacan's principles theoretical models that are useful to feminist praxis.

2. In another text, Lacan describes language determining human consciousness in terms of language's symbolic value: "Man speaks, then, but it is because the symbol has made him man" (Lacan, *Ecrits* 65).

3. Francis Jacques is aware that many languages have no specific apparatus for constructing third-person pronouns, but he feels that these languages still leave room for the perception of the third person: "It is quite true that certain languages seem to give no explicit recognition to the third person; instead, there is simply an absence of the formal markers for the first and second persons. But the tendency among linguists is to stress the heteogeneity [sic] of the three persons" (34).

4. The construction of the child reader's subjectivity, influenced as it must be by a narrative's ideological machinations, is a separate issue. I refer the reader to John Stephens's excellent analysis of this process in chapter 2 of *Language and Ideology in Children's Fiction*.

5. For a more detailed explanation of Arthur's developing perception of his own subjectivity, I refer the reader to my article, "Claiming the Treasures: Patricia MacLachlan's Organic Postmodernism."

6. Anna Altmann contrasts parodic and nonparodic feminist fairy-tale picture books, but her definition of nonparodic feminist fairy tales applies quite smoothly to *The Magical Adventures of Pretty Pearl*, *Weetzie Bat*, and *The Tricksters*. These texts all "offer a new and wider world of meaning through reconfigured events and characters" ("Parody" 23); they are "about what women can be and are, not about how women have been constructed in the past. . . . Their challenge to constricting gender roles is made within the form of the fairy tale, by creating a new vision rather than contesting

the old" ("Parody" 28). Thus, according to Altmann's terms, these three novels are feminist fairy tales.

7. My ideas here have been influenced by Lissa Paul's manuscript "Coming Second Second Coming: Engendering Theories about Children's Books."

8. Aladdin has the same basic conversation with the genie in the Disney movie, released in 1992, three years after the publication of *Weetzie Bat*.

4. TRANSFORMING FEMININE SILENCE

Portions of this chapter first appeared as an article, "Is Flying Extraordinary? Patricia MacLachlan's Use of Aporia," *Children's Literature* 23 (1995): 202–20.

1. Studies by Sally L. Kitch, Marianne Hirsch, Janis P. Stout, and Brenda O. Daly and Maureen T. Reddy also treat specific literary instances of the silencing of women.

2. For more on aporia and silencing in MacLachlan's *Unclaimed Treasures* and *The Facts and Fictions of Minna Pratt* (1988), see my article, "Is Flying Extraordinary? Patricia MacLachlan's Use of Aporia."

3. Mary Field Belenky et al. might describe these characters' growth as a move from the stage wherein a female defines reality by listening to authoritarian voices to the stage wherein she develops a capacity for determining reality by listening to her own inner, subjective voice (54–55). Unlike many psychologists who set up age-driven paradigms, Belenky et al. note that a female's development from living according to "received knowledge" to living according to "subjective knowledge" can occur at any age (55). Certainly not the pinnacle of female development, a reliance on subjective knowledge represents at least a stage of intellectual autonomy on the path to a stage wherein the female can integrate the voices of many people in constructing her own perceptions (133–35).

Belenky et al., as well as Brown and Gilligan, demonstrate the primacy of language and voice to the female's developing sense of self (Belenky et al. 3–20; Brown and Gilligan 216–18).

4. Belenky et al. note that dichotomous thinking is endemic to the stage wherein females turn to authoritarian voices for answers: women in this stage "assume that there is only one right answer to each question, and that all other answers and all contrary views are automatically wrong" (37).

5. Janice M. Alberghene notes how MacLachlan deals with the traditional Cartesian split between mind and body: "For MacLachlan, mind and body are no more opposites than are fact and fiction (or for that matter, reason

and imagination); they are complements. Thought and imagination extend the body's knowing" ("The Stories" 4–5).

6. When Rosellen Brown reviewed *Baby* in the *New York Times Book Review*, she alluded to some of the text's other fairy-tale qualities. Of the adults in *Baby* she writes, "superbly mature and articulate people play the roles assigned, in more primitive times, to fairy godmothers," and she notes how much like a "fairy child" Sophie is (34).

5. RE/CONSTRUCTING THE FEMALE WRITER

1. One significant problem that Jo March faces is this lack of an encouraging mentor; her mentor figure, Professor Bhaer, actually discourages her writing. Beverly Lyon Clark catalogs the "devaluation" of writing that occurs throughout the novel (90).

2. Lissa Paul asserts that "Ole Golly usually doesn't quite understand what she reads. She quotes a lot, but can't explain the quotations" ("Feminist Writers" 67–68). Nevertheless, although Ole Golly can't fully explain Dostoievsky (as Francis Molson has noted ["Another Look" 966]), the complete appropriateness of Ole Golly's use of Keats indicates that she does, in fact, understand this particular quotation and that she is intentionally and accurately applying it to a pertinent context.

3. Paul points out that Alcott achieves, in a sense, a sort of subversive victory with *Little Women* in that even though Jo gives up her identity as writer, it is still Jo-the-writer, the rebellious character of the first two thirds of the book, who remains alive in readers' memories ("Coming Second," chap. 8). On the other hand, Estes and Lant call the ending of *Little Women* a "spiritual murder" (103), a "desperate mutilation" of both Jo and the text itself (116), as Alcott grafts onto Jo Beth's compliant characteristics to transform the rebellious young writer into the image of Victorian domesticity.

4. In her acceptance speech of the 1992 Phoenix award at the Nineteenth International Children's Literature Association Conference in Hartford, Connecticut, Hunter stated that everything that happened in *Sound of Chariots* really happened to her when she was a child.

5. Note, too, that Leigh's mother struggles and succeeds at building a life for herself and her son after her divorce. She does not perceive herself as a victim because the divorce has been her choice.

6. FEMALE INTERDEPENDENCY

1. The same can be said of men, too: true community exists in any

group only if each member of the community recognizes and is allowed to recognize his or her agency.

2. Hamilton has a knack for revising Freudian symbols and reclaiming them for feminism. Near the end of *Justice and Her Brothers* (1972), Justice participates in a Great Snake Race with her brothers and the boys in their neighborhood. Misunderstanding the rules of the race, Justice catches the biggest snake she can find instead of catching the most snakes. Thinking that she has lost, Justice opens her bag the next morning to find over a hundred snakes, for her snake has given birth. The snake is transformed from a phallic to a maternal symbol, and maternity is shown to have the greater strength of the two since it ultimately triumphs in this race.

3. Hamilton identifies her "ideas of community, and I suppose socialism really, living in a communal way" as part of what makes M. C. special to her (Mikkelsen 394).

4. Virginia Schaffer Carroll provides a feminist reinterpretation of *Seventeenth Summer* in her essay "Re-Reading the Romance of *Seventeenth Summer*."

5. Although *The Wings of a Falcon* focuses on the friendship between two males, by the time Beryl enters the text in the final third of the narrative, Voigt's feminist agenda is clear. The boys have already encountered a transvestite woman who poses as a man to gain power in her community, and Beryl teaches them to treat women as equals. In the final dialogue of the book she says, "I will speak when I have something to say. What is this *must*? What I must have is the right to decide when I have something to say, and when I do not, that is my must. Otherwise, I am no more than a puppet, if you can pull the string and I *must* have words in my mouth" (466). And most important of all: the gender of Beryl's child (who will be the next ruler of the Kingdom) is never revealed. The text's silence on this issue implies that gender is immaterial.

6. Published only months before the Anita Hill/Clarence Thomas hearings, *Lyddie* proved to be a timely commentary on sexual harassment.

7. REFUTING FREUD

Portions of this chapter first appeared as an article, "Nesting: Embedded Narratives as Maternal Discourse in Children's Novels," *Children's Literature Association Quarterly* 18 (1993–94): 165–70.

1. Lacan posits the notion of the Imaginary as a stage in which the child imagines itself to be completely unified with its mother. This stage is "pre-Oedipal" because the child has not yet entered the conflict of the mother's attention that defines the Oedipal stage. The recognition that the child and mother are separate entities marks the child's initiation into the Symbolic

Order. For a concise explanation of Lacan's sometimes dense prose, see Natov (2–3).

2. Trudy Krisher's *Spite Fences* (1994) is an example of a text that *does* explore why a neurotic mother is so damaging to her daughter.

3. The novel gains much of its power by virtue of the fact that it is a roman à clef. Crescent Dragonwagon is the daughter of Charlotte Zolotow, long a prestigious children's book editor at Harper and Row. Although the adolescent reader might not know the significance of all the personalities involved, the reader will recognize the genuineness of the voice writing the narrative.

4. The image of maternal connection is as markedly Gilligan-like as the rope ladder that connects the Killburn families in *M. C. Higgins the Great*.

5. Gates uses "signification" as a homonym that "both enact[s] and recapitulate[s] the received, classic confrontation between Afro-American culture and American culture. . . . The relationship that black 'Signification' bears to the English 'signification' is, paradoxically, a relation of difference inscribed within a relation of identity" (45). Gates maintains of signification that "it is in the vernacular that, since slavery, the black person has encoded private yet communal cultural rituals" (xix).

6. For further analysis of feminist nested narratives, see my article "Nesting: Embedded Narratives as Maternal Discourse in Children's Novels."

7. This is not to say that nonfeminist writers avoid circularity. Nonlinearity has been part of the narrative tradition since its inception. But Greene details the ways that metafiction, self-referentiality, and structural and imagistic notions of circularity are particularly strong concerns for feminist novelists.

8. Waugh defines novels of realism as those which tend to ignore the fact that they are constructs by pretending that the worlds they create are "real," thereby suppressing the dialogue between discourses that Bakhtin defines as the shaping force of the novel (Waugh, *Metafictions* 5–6). Traditional children's realism is especially likely to maintain this illusion of reality.

9. The assumption that children prefer straightforward, linear plots to more involved plots is a misconception common especially among pedagogical critics of children's literature. One obvious example comes from the fifth edition of Charlotte S. Huck, Susan Hepler, and Janet Hickman's college-level textbook, *Children's Literature in the Elementary School*: "Most plots in children's literature are presented in a linear fashion. Frequently, children find it confusing to follow several plot lines or to deal with flashbacks in time and place" (21). The authors then go on to contradict themselves by providing successful examples of books with nonlinear plots: Robert O'Brien's *Mrs. Frisby and the Rats of NIMH* and Virginia Hamilton's *Cousins.*

10. Having two settings in time allows the reader to experience more than one subject position: that of the narrator in the framing tale and that of the narrator in the framed tale. According to Steven Cohan and Linda M. Shires, such shifts in subjectivity minimize the ideological effect of a straightforward linear narrative that has only one narrative voice. Linear narratives may lull the reader into temporarily accepting their ideology by implying that only one possible ideological position exists for the reader to adopt; the embedded narrative structure provides for the possibility of at least two subject positions from which to interpret the text's ideology (Cohan and Shires 170–75). In the nested narrative of maternal discourse, the dual subject position is vital in allowing the reader to experience the ideological subject position of both the maternal and the daughter figure.

11. Brown and Gilligan also suggest that connections between women and girls are necessary for the psychological health of both groups (216–17).

8. METAFICTION AND THE POLITICS OF IDENTITY

1. John Stephens's definition of metafiction is similar to Moss's; he calls it "the strategy of suspending the illusion of fiction in some way in order to direct attention to the processes of making fiction" ("Metafiction" 101).

2. Le Guin describes her developing feminism in "Is Gender Necessary? Redux."

3. In other words, in this language there is no separation between an object and the word it represents. Spoken languages have a largely arbitrary relationship between a word (or "signifier") and the object it represents (the "signified"); the word "c-a-t," for example, has no direct relationship to the actual animal. But in Le Guin's fantasy world, no such arbitrary linguistic relationship exists in the language of the dragons.

4. Kalessin's gender is intentionally obscure in *Tehanu*; in *The Farthest Shore*, the point is made that "whether Kalessin was male or female, there was no telling" (219).

5. See, for example, Alice Walker's definition of "womanism" in *In Search of Our Mothers' Gardens* (xi–xii) or Barbara Smith's "Racism and Women's Studies."

9. AFTERWORD

1. For my analysis of how the morality, images, and themes are even more sexist in Disney's than in Andersen's *Little Mermaid*, see my "Disney's Sub/Version of Andersen's *Little Mermaid*."

BIBLIOGRAPHY

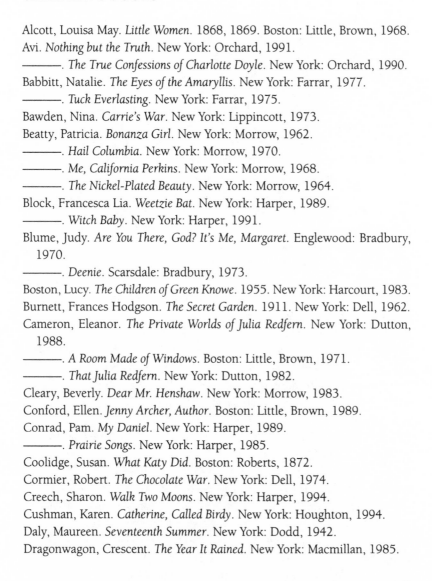

CHILDREN'S BOOKS

Alcott, Louisa May. *Little Women*. 1868, 1869. Boston: Little, Brown, 1968.

Avi. *Nothing but the Truth*. New York: Orchard, 1991.

———. *The True Confessions of Charlotte Doyle*. New York: Orchard, 1990.

Babbitt, Natalie. *The Eyes of the Amaryllis*. New York: Farrar, 1977.

———. *Tuck Everlasting*. New York: Farrar, 1975.

Bawden, Nina. *Carrie's War*. New York: Lippincott, 1973.

Beatty, Patricia. *Bonanza Girl*. New York: Morrow, 1962.

———. *Hail Columbia*. New York: Morrow, 1970.

———. *Me, California Perkins*. New York: Morrow, 1968.

———. *The Nickel-Plated Beauty*. New York: Morrow, 1964.

Block, Francesca Lia. *Weetzie Bat*. New York: Harper, 1989.

———. *Witch Baby*. New York: Harper, 1991.

Blume, Judy. *Are You There, God? It's Me, Margaret*. Englewood: Bradbury, 1970.

———. *Deenie*. Scarsdale: Bradbury, 1973.

Boston, Lucy. *The Children of Green Knowe*. 1955. New York: Harcourt, 1983.

Burnett, Frances Hodgson. *The Secret Garden*. 1911. New York: Dell, 1962.

Cameron, Eleanor. *The Private Worlds of Julia Redfern*. New York: Dutton, 1988.

———. *A Room Made of Windows*. Boston: Little, Brown, 1971.

———. *That Julia Redfern*. New York: Dutton, 1982.

Cleary, Beverly. *Dear Mr. Henshaw*. New York: Morrow, 1983.

Conford, Ellen. *Jenny Archer, Author*. Boston: Little, Brown, 1989.

Conrad, Pam. *My Daniel*. New York: Harper, 1989.

———. *Prairie Songs*. New York: Harper, 1985.

Coolidge, Susan. *What Katy Did*. Boston: Roberts, 1872.

Cormier, Robert. *The Chocolate War*. New York: Dell, 1974.

Creech, Sharon. *Walk Two Moons*. New York: Harper, 1994.

Cushman, Karen. *Catherine, Called Birdy*. New York: Houghton, 1994.

Daly, Maureen. *Seventeenth Summer*. New York: Dodd, 1942.

Dragonwagon, Crescent. *The Year It Rained*. New York: Macmillan, 1985.

Edgeworth, Maria. "Rivuletta." *Early Lessons*. 2 vols. 1801. Rpt. London: 1815. 2:79–95. Opie Collection 2:138.

Engdahl, Sylvia. *Enchantress from the Stars*. New York: Macmillan, 1970.

Fitzhugh, Louise. *Harriet the Spy*. New York: Dell, 1964.

Fleischman, Paul. *The Borning Room*. New York: Harper, 1991.

Fleischman, Sid. *The Whipping Boy*. New York: Greenwillow, 1986.

Garden, Nancy. *Annie on My Mind*. New York: Farrar, 1982.

George, Jean. *Julie of the Wolves*. New York: Harper, 1972.

Greenwald, Sheila. *It All Began with Jane Eyre*. Boston: Little, Brown, 1980.

———. *Rosy Cole Discovers America*. Boston: Joy Street, 1992.

———. *Rosy's Romance*. Boston: Joy Street, 1989.

Guy, Rosa. *Edith Jackson*. Viking, 1978.

———. *The Friends*. New York: Holt, 1973.

Hamilton, Virginia. *Arilla Sun Down*. New York: Greenwillow, 1976.

———. *Cousins*. New York: Philomel, 1990.

———. *Justice and Her Brothers*. New York: Greenwillow, 1972.

———. *The Magical Adventures of Pretty Pearl*. New York: Harper, 1983.

———. *M. C. Higgins the Great*. New York: Macmillan, 1974.

———. *Plain City*. New York: Scholastic, 1993.

———. *The Planet of Junior Brown*. New York: Macmillan, 1971.

———. *A White Romance*. New York: Philomel, 1987.

———. *Zeely*. New York: Macmillan, 1967.

Hinton, S. E. *The Outsiders*. New York: Viking, 1967.

Ho, Minfong. *Rice without Rain*. London: Deutsch, 1986.

Hope, Laura Lee. *The Bobbsey Twins: Merry Days Indoors and Out*. 1904. Rpt. Racine: Whitman, 1950.

Hunt, Irene. *Up a Road Slowly*. New York: Grosset, 1968.

Hunter, Mollie. *A Sound of Chariots*. 1972. New York: HarperTrophy, 1988.

Johnson, Angela. *Toning the Sweep*. New York: Orchard, 1993.

Kalman, Maira. *Max Makes a Million*. New York: Viking, 1990.

Kerr, M. E. *Dinkey Hocker Shoots Smack*. New York: Harper, 1972.

Kincaid, Jamaica. *Annie John*. New York: Farrar, 1983.

Konigsburg, E. L. *From the Mixed-Up Files of Mrs. Basil E. Frankweiler*. New York: Dell, 1967.

Krisher, Trudy. *Spite Fences*. New York: Delacorte, 1994.

Le Guin, Ursula K. *The Farthest Shore*. New York: Atheneum, 1972.

———. *Tehanu: The Last Book of Earthsea*. New York: Macmillan, 1990.

Little, Jean. *Look through My Window*. New York: Harper, 1970.

Lowry, Lois. *Anastasia Krupnik*. New York: Dutton, 1979.

Lunn, Janet. *The Root Cellar*. New York: Scribner, 1983.

———. *Shadow in Hawthorn Bay*. Toronto: Puffin, 1988.

Macaulay, David. *Black and White*. Boston: Houghton, 1990.

MacLachlan, Patricia. *Arthur, for the Very First Time*. New York: Harper, 1980.

———. *Baby*. New York: Delacorte, 1993.

———. *Cassie Binegar*. New York: Harper, 1982.

———. *The Facts and Fictions of Minna Pratt*. New York: Harper, 1988.

———. *Journey*. New York: Delacorte, 1991.

———. *Sarah, Plain and Tall*. New York: Harper, 1985.

———. *Unclaimed Treasures*. New York: Harper, 1984.

Mahy, Margaret. *The Changeover*. New York: Scholastic, 1984.

———. *The Tricksters*. New York: McElderry, 1986.

Matas, Carol. *The Burning Time*. New York: Delacorte, 1994.

McKinley, Robin. *The Blue Sword*. New York: Greenwillow, 1982.

———. *The Hero and the Crown*. New York: Greenwillow, 1985.

Mohr, Nicholasa. *Nilda*. New York: Harper, 1973.

Montgomery, Lucy Maud. *Anne of Green Gables*. Boston: Page, 1908.

Norton, Mary. *The Borrowers*. New York: Harcourt, 1953.

O'Brien, Robert. *Mrs. Frisby and the Rats of NIMH*. New York: Philomel, 1971.

Paterson, Katherine. *Jacob Have I Loved*. New York: Crowell, 1980.

———. *Lyddie*. New York: Dutton, 1991.

Rylant, Cynthia. *Missing May*. New York: Orchard, 1992.

Scieszka, Jon. *The Stinky Cheese Man and Other Fairly Stupid Tales*. Illus. Lane Smith. New York: Scholastic, 1993.

Smith, Betty. *A Tree Grows in Brooklyn*. New York: Harper, 1943.

Spinelli, Jerry. *Maniac Magee*. Boston: Little, 1990.

———. *There's a Girl in My Hammerlock*. New York: Simon, 1991.

Taylor, Mildred. *Let the Circle Be Unbroken*. New York: Dial, 1981.

———. *The Road to Memphis*. New York: Dial, 1990.

———. *Roll of Thunder, Hear My Cry*. New York: Dial, 1976.

Voigt, Cynthia. *Dicey's Song*. New York: Atheneum, 1982.

———. *The Homecoming*. New York: Atheneum, 1981.

———. *Jackaroo*. New York: Atheneum, 1985.

———. *On Fortune's Wheel*. New York: Atheneum, 1990.

———. *Tell Me if the Lovers Are Losers*. New York: Atheneum, 1982.

———. *When She Hollers*. New York: Scholastic, 1994.

———. *The Wings of a Falcon*. New York: Scholastic, 1993.

Webster, Jean. *Daddy-Long-Legs*. 1912. New York: Penguin, 1989.

Wersba, Barbara. *Fat: A Love Story*. New York: Harper, 1987.

———. *Love Is the Crooked Thing*. New York: Harper, 1987.

White, E. B. *Charlotte's Web*. New York: Harper, 1952.

Wilder, Laura Ingalls. *The Little House in the Big Woods*. New York: Harper, 1932.

———. *These Happy Golden Years*. Eau Claire: Hale, 1943.

Yep, Lawrence. *Dragonwings*. New York: Harper, 1975.

Zindel, Paul. *The Pigman*. New York: Harper, 1968.

CRITICAL WORKS

Abel, Elizabeth, Marianne Hirsch, and Elizabeth Langland. *The Voyage In: Fictions of Female Development*. Hanover: UP of New England, 1983.

Aippersbach, Kim. "*Tuck Everlasting* and the Tree at the Center of the World." *Children's Literature in Education* 21 (1990): 83–97.

Alberghene, Janice Marie. *From Alcott to Abel's Island: The Image of the Artist in American Children's Literature*. Ph.D. diss. Brown University, 1980.

———. "The Stories of Patricia MacLachlan, Plain and Tall: A Paper in Two Parts." Nineteenth Annual Children's Literature Association International Conference, Hartford, Conn., June 5, 1992.

Altmann, Anna E. "Parody and Poesis in Feminist Fairy Tales." *Canadian Children's Literature* 73 (1994): 22–31.

———. "Welding Brass Tits on the Armor: An Examination of the Quest Metaphor in Robin McKinley's *The Hero and the Crown*." *Children's Literature in Education* 23 (1992): 143–56.

Auerbach, Nina. *Communities of Women: An Idea in Fiction*. Cambridge: Harvard UP, 1978.

———. *Woman and the Demon: The Life of a Victorian Myth*. Cambridge: Harvard UP, 1982.

Bakhtin, Mikhail. *The Dialogic Imagination: Four Essays by M. M. Bakhtin*. Ed. Michael Holquist, trans. Caryl Emerson and Michael Holquist. Austin: U of Texas P, 1981.

Bal, Mieke. *Narratology: Introduction to the Theory of Narrative*. Trans. Christine van Boheemen. Toronto: U of Toronto P, 1985.

Bauer, Dale. *Feminist Dialogics: A Theory of Failed Community*. Albany: State U of New York P, 1988.

Belenky, Mary Field, Blythe McVicker Clinchy, Nancy Rule Goldberger, and Jill Mattuck Tarule. *Women's Ways of Knowing: The Development of Self, Voice, and Mind*. New York: Basic, 1986.

Belsey, Catherine. "Constructing the Subject: Deconstructing the Text." *Feminist Criticism and Social Change*. Ed. J. Newton and D. Rosenfelt. London: Methuen, 1985. 45–64.

———. *Critical Practice*. New York: Routledge, 1980.

Benveniste, Emile. *Problems in General Linguistics*. Miami: U of Miami P, 1971.

Bottigheimer, Ruth. *Grimms' Bad Girls and Bold Boys: The Moral and Social Vision of the Tales.* New Haven: Yale UP, 1987.

Brown, Lyn Mikel, and Carol Gilligan. *Meeting at the Crossroads: Women's Psychology and Girls' Development.* Cambridge: Harvard UP, 1992.

Brown, Rosellen. "On Loan: One Little Sister." Review of *Baby* by Patricia MacLachlan. *New York Times Book Review,* November 14, 1993, 34.

Butler, Judith. *Gender Trouble: Feminism and the Subversion of Identity.* New York: Routledge, 1990.

Cadogan, Mary, and Patricia Craig. *You're a Brick, Angela! A New Look at Girls' Fiction from 1839–1975.* London: Gollancz, 1976.

Carroll, Virginia Schaffer. "Re-Reading the Romance of *Seventeenth Summer.*" *Children's Literature Association Quarterly* 21 (1996): 12–19.

Chodorow, Nancy. *The Reproduction of Mothering.* Berkeley: U of California P, 1978.

Christ, Carol. *Diving Deep and Surfacing: Woman Writers on Spiritual Quest.* Boston: Beacon, 1980.

Cixous, Hélène. "Castration or Decapitation?" *Signs* 7 (1981): 41–55.

———. "The Laugh of the Medusa." *Signs* 1 (Summer 1976): 875–93.

Cixous, Hélène, and C. Clement. *The Newly Born Woman.* Trans. Betsy Wing. Manchester: Manchester UP, 1986.

Clark, Beverly Lyon. "A Portrait of the Artist as a Little Woman." *Children's Literature* 17 (1989): 81–97.

Cohan, Steven, and Linda M. Shires. *Telling Stories: A Theoretical Analysis of Narrative Fiction.* New York: Routledge, 1988.

Daly, Brenda O., and Maureen T. Reddy. *Narrating Mothers: Theorizing Maternal Subjectivities.* Knoxville: U of Tennessee P, 1991.

De Beauvoir, Simone. *The Second Sex.* 1949. Trans. and ed. H. M. Parshley. New York: Knopf, 1974.

de Man, Paul. *Allegories of Reading.* New Haven: Yale UP, 1979.

Derrida, Jacques. *Writing and Difference.* Trans. Alan Bass. Chicago: U of Chicago P, 1978.

Dixon, Bob. *Catching Them Young 1: Sex, Race, and Class in Children's Fiction.* London: Pluto, 1977.

———. *Catching Them Young 2: Political Ideas in Children's Fiction.* London: Pluto, 1977.

Estes, Angela M., and Kathleen M. Lant. "Dismembering the Text: The Horror of Louisa May Alcott's *Little Women.*" *Children's Literature* 17 (1989): 98–123.

Fellman, Anita Clair. "Laura Ingalls Wilder and Rose Wilder Lane: The Politics of a Mother-Daughter Relationship." *Signs* 15 (1990): 535–61.

Felman, Shoshana. *Literature and Psychoanalysis: The Question of Reading: Otherwise*. Baltimore: Johns Hopkins UP, 1982.

Flynn, Gail. "Placelessness in *Jacob Have I Loved*." Twenty-First Annual Children's Literature Association International Conference, Springfield, Mo., June 5, 1994.

Fox, Mem. "Men Who Weep, Boys Who Dance: The Gender Agenda between the Lines in Children's Literature." *Language Arts* 70 (1993): 84–88.

French, Marilyn. *Beyond Power: On Women, Men, and Morals*. New York: Summit, 1985.

Friday, Nancy. *My Mother/My Self: The Daughter's Search for Identity*. New York: Delacorte, 1977.

Friedman, Susan Stanford. "Creativity and the Childbirth Metaphor: Gender Difference in Literary Discourse." *Feminist Studies* 13.1 (1987): 49–82.

Fuss, Diana. *Essentially Speaking: Feminism, Nature, and Difference*. New York: Routledge, 1989.

Gallop, Jane. *Thinking through the Body*. New York: Columbia UP, 1988.

Gates, Henry Louis, Jr. *The Signifying Monkey: A Theory of African-American Literary Criticism*. New York: Oxford UP, 1988.

Gibson, Lois Rauch. "Beyond the Apron: Archetypes, Stereotypes, and Alternative Portrayals of Mothers in Children's Literature." *Children's Literature Association Quarterly* 13 (1988): 177–81.

Gilbert, Sandra, and Susan Gubar. *The Madwoman in the Attic: The Woman Writer and the Nineteenth-Century Literary Imagination*. New Haven: Yale UP, 1979.

Gilligan, Carol. *In a Different Voice: Psychological Theory and Women's Development*. Cambridge: Harvard UP, 1982.

Goodman, Jan. "Lesbian and Gay Characters in Children's Literature." *Interracial Books for Children Bulletin* 14.3–4 (1983): 13–15.

Gravitt, Sandra. "'We Dance to the Music of Our Own Times': Reflected Images of Granddaughters and Grandmothers." *The Image of the Child in Children's Literature: Proceedings of the 1991 International Conference of the Children's Literature Association*. Ed. Sylvia Patterson Iskander. Battle Creek: Children's Literature Association, 1991. 120–26.

Greene, Gayle. *Changing the Story: Feminist Fiction and the Tradition*. Bloomington: Indiana UP, 1991.

Harris, Violet. *Teaching Multicultural Literature in Grades K–8*. Norwood: Christopher-Gordon, 1992.

Hatfield, Len. "From Master to Brother: Shifting the Balance of Authority in Ursula K. Le Guin's *Farthest Shore* and *Tehanu*." *Children's Literature* 21 (1993): 43–65.

Heilbrun, Carolyn. "Silence and Women's Voices." *Women's Voices*. Ed. Lorna Duphiney Edmundson, Judith P. Saunders, and Ellen S. Silber. Littleton: Copley, 1987. 4–12.

———. *Toward a Recognition of Androgyny*. New York: Knopf, 1973.

———. *Writing a Woman's Life*. New York: Norton, 1988.

Hirsch, Marianne. *The Mother/Daughter Plot: Narrative, Psychoanalysis, Feminism*. Bloomington: Indiana UP, 1989.

———. "Spiritual *Bildung*: The Beautiful Soul as Paradigm." *The Voyage In: Fictions of Female Development*. Ed. Elizabeth Abel, Marianne Hirsch, and Elizabeth Langland. Hanover: UP of New England, 1983. 23–48.

Hollindale, Peter. "Ideology and the Children's Book." *Signal* 55 (1988): 3–22.

hooks, bell. *Ain't I a Woman: Black Women and Feminism*. Boston: South End Press, 1981.

Huck, Charlotte S., Susan Hepler, and Janet Hickman. *Children's Literature in the Elementary School*, 5th ed. Fort Worth: Harcourt, 1993.

Hunt, Peter. *Criticism, Theory, and Children's Literature*. Cambridge: Basil Blackwell, 1991.

Jacques, Francis. *Difference and Subjectivity: Dialogue and Personal Identity*. Trans. Andrew Rothwell. New Haven: Yale UP, 1991.

Jefferson, Ann. "*Mise en abyme* and the Prophetic in Narrative." *Style* 17.2 (Spring 1983): 196–208.

Johnson, Barbara. *A World of Difference*. Baltimore: Johns Hopkins UP, 1987.

Johnson, Dianne. "'I See Me in the Book': Visual Literacy and African-American Children's Literature." *Children's Literature Association Quarterly* 15 (1990): 10–14.

———. *Telling Tales: The Pedagogy and Promise of African American Literature for Youth*. New York: Greenwood, 1990.

Kaminer, Wendy. "Feminism's Identity Crisis." *Atlantic* (October 1993): 51–68.

Kerferd, G. B. *The Sophistic Movement*. Cambridge: Cambridge UP, 1981.

Kertzer, Adrienne. "This Quiet Lady: Maternal Voices and the Picture Book." *Children's Literature Association Quarterly* 18 (1993–94): 159–64.

Key, Mary Ritchie. "The Role of Male and Female in Children's Books: Dispelling All Doubt." *Wilson Library Bulletin* 46 (1971): 167–76.

Keyser, Elizabeth Lennox. "Alcott's Portraits of the Artist as Little Woman." *International Journal of Women's Studies* 5 (1982): 445–59.

Kitch, Sally L. "Gender and Language: Dialect, Silence and the Disruption of Discourse." *Women's Studies* 14 (1987): 65–78.

Kolodny, Annette. "Dancing through the Minefield: Some Observations on the Theory, Practice, and Politics of a Feminist Literary Criticism." *Feminist Studies* 6.1 (1980): 1–25.

Kortenhaus, Carole M., and Jack Demarest. "Gender Role Stereotyping in Children's Literature: An Update." *Sex Roles* 28 (1993): 219–32.

Kristeva, Julia. *Desire in Language: A Semiotic Approach to Literature and Art.* New York: Columbia UP, 1980.

———. "Women's Time." *Signs* 7 (Autumn 1981): 13–35.

Kuznets, Lois Rostow. *When Toys Come Alive: Narratives of Animation, Metamorphosis, and Development.* New Haven: Yale UP, 1994.

Lacan, Jacques. *Ecrits: A Selection.* Trans. Alan Sheridan. New York: Norton, 1977.

———. *Feminine Sexuality.* Trans. Jacqueline Rose, ed. Juliet Mitchell and Jacqueline Rose. New York: Norton, 1982.

———. *The Four Fundamental Concepts of Psycho-Analysis.* Trans. Alan Sheridan, ed. Jacques-Alain Miller. New York: Norton, 1978.

Langerman, Deborah. "Books and Boys: Gender Preferences and Book Selection." *School Library Journal* 36 (1990): 132–36.

Le Guin, Ursula K. "Is Gender Necessary? Redux." *Dancing at the Edge of the World: Thoughts on Words, Women, Places.* New York: Harper, 1989. 7–16.

Lewis, David. "The Constructedness of Texts: Picture Books and the Metafictive." *Signal* 62 (May 1990): 131–46.

Lurie, Alison. *Don't Tell the Grownups! Subversive Children's Literature.* Boston: Little, Brown, 1990.

MacCann, Donnarae, and Gloria Woodard, eds. *The Black American in Books for Children.* Metuchen: Scarecrow, 1972.

———. *Cultural Conformity in Books for Children: Further Readings in Racism.* Metuchen: Scarecrow, 1977.

MacCannell, Juliet Flower. *Figuring Lacan: Criticism and the Cultural Unconscious.* Lincoln: U of Nebraska P, 1987.

MacLachlan, Patricia. "Newbery Medal Acceptance." *Horn Book* 62 (1986): 407–13.

McGillis, Roderick. "'Secrets' and 'Sequence' in Children's Stories." *Studies in the Literary Imagination* 18.2 (1985): 35–46.

McKay, Nellie. "Reflections on Black Women Writers: Revising the Literary Canon." *The Impact of Feminist Research in the Academy.* Ed. Christie Farnham. Bloomington: Indiana UP, 1987. 174–89.

Michel, Andrée. *Down with Stereotypes! Eliminating Sexism from Children's Literature.* Paris: UNESCO, 1986.

Mikkelsen, Nina. "A Conversation with Virginia Hamilton." *Journal of Youth Library Services* 7 (1994): 392–405.

Miller, Nancy K., ed. *The Poetics of Gender*. New York: Columbia UP, 1986.

Minh-Ha, Trinh T. *When the Moon Waxes Red: Representation, Gender, and Cultural Politics*. New York: Routledge, 1991.

Moers, Ellen. *Literary Women*. New York: Doubleday, 1976.

Moi, Toril. *Sexual/Textual Politics*. London: Methuen, 1986.

Molson, Francis J. "Another Look at *Harriet the Spy*." *Elementary English* 51 (1974): 963–70.

———. "Portrait of the Young Writer in Children's Fiction." *Lion and the Unicorn* 1 (1977): 77–90.

Moss, Anita. "Feminist Criticism and the Study of Children's Literature." *Children's Literature Association Quarterly* 7.4 (1982): 3–22.

———. "Frontiers of Gender in Children's Literature: Virginia Hamilton's *Arilla Sun Down*." *Children's Literature Association Quarterly* 8 (1983): 25–27.

———. "Varieties of Children's Metafiction." *Studies in the Literary Imagination* 18.2 (1985): 79–92.

Moss, Geoff. "Metafiction and the Poetics of Children's Literature." *Children's Literature Association Quarterly* 15 (1990): 50–52.

Mowder, Louise. "Domestication of Desire: Gender, Language, and Landscape in the Little House Books." *Children's Literature Association Quarterly* 17 (1992): 15–19.

Myers, Mitzi. "The Dilemmas of Gender as Double-Voiced Narrative; or, Maria Edgeworth Mothers the Bildungsroman." *The Idea of the Novel in the Eighteenth Century*. Ed. Robert Uphaus. East Lansing: Colleagues, 1988. 67–96.

———. "Impeccable Governesses, Rational Dames, and Moral Mothers: Mary Wollstonecraft and the Female Tradition in Georgian Children's Books." *Children's Literature* 14 (1986): 31–59.

Natov, Roni. "Mothers and Daughters: Jamaica Kincaid's Pre-Oedipal Narrative." *Children's Literature* 18 (1990): 1–16.

Nieto, Sonia. "Children's Literature on Puerto Rican Themes." *Interracial Books for Children Bulletin* 14.1–2 (1983): 6–9.

Nilsen, Alleen Pace. "Women in Children's Literature." *College English* 32 (1972): 918–26.

Nodelman, Perry. "Children's Literature as Women's Writing." *Children's Literature Association Quarterly* 13 (1988): 31–34.

———. "How Typical Children Read Typical Books." *Children's Literature in Education* 12 (1977): 177–85.

Parry, Sally. "The Secret of the Patriarchal System: The Search for Values in Nancy Drew and Judy Bolton." Unpublished manuscript.

Paul, Lissa. "Coming Second Second Coming: Engendering Theories about Children's Books." Unpublished manuscript.

————. "Enigma Variations: What Feminist Theory Knows about Children's Literature." *Signal* 54 (September 1987): 186–201.

————. "The Feminist Writer as Heroine in *Harriet the Spy*." *Lion and the Unicorn* 13 (1989): 67–73.

Pratt, Annis. *Archetypal Patterns in Women's Fiction*. Bloomington: Indiana UP, 1981.

Reinstein, P. Gila. "Sex Roles in Recent Picture Books." *Journal of Popular Culture* 17 (1984): 116–23.

Rich, Adrienne. *Of Woman Born: Motherhood as Experience and Institution*. New York: Norton, 1976.

————. "When We Dead Awaken: Writing as Re-Vision." *On Lies, Secrets, and Silence: Selected Prose, 1966–1978*. New York: Norton, 1979.

Rose, Ellen Cronan. "Through the Looking Glass: When Women Tell Fairy-Tales." *The Voyage In: Fictions of Female Development*. Ed. Elizabeth Abel, Marianne Hirsch, and Elizabeth Langland. Hanover: UP of New England, 1983. 209–27.

Schon, Isabel. "Good and Bad Books about Hispanic People and Culture for Young Readers." *Multicultural Review* 2.1 (1993): 28–31.

Schweickart, Patrocinio. "Reading Ourselves: Toward a Feminist Theory of Reading." *Gender and Reading: Essays on Readers, Texts, and Contexts*. Ed. Elizabeth A. Flynn and Patrocinio P. Schweickart. Baltimore: Johns Hopkins UP, 1986. 31–62.

Showalter, Elaine. "Feminist Criticism in the Wilderness." *Critical Inquiry* 8.1 (1981): 179–205.

————. *A Literature of Their Own*. Princeton: Princeton UP, 1977.

————. *Sister's Choice: Tradition and Change in American Women's Writing*. New York: Oxford UP, 1991.

Sims, Rudine. *Shadow and Substance: Afro-American Experience in Contemporary Children's Fiction*. Urbana: NCTE, 1982.

Smedman, M. Sarah. "Not Always Gladly Does She Teach, nor Gladly Learn: Teachers in *Künstlerinroman* for Young Readers." *Children's Literature in Education* 20 (1989): 131–49.

Smith, Barbara. "Racism and Women's Studies." *All the Women Are White, All the Blacks Are Men, But Some of Us Are Brave: Black Women's Studies*. Ed. Gloria T. Hull, Patricia Bell Scott, and Barbara Smith. Old Westbury: Feminist Press, 1982.

Spacks, Patricia Meyer. *The Female Imagination*. New York: Knopf, 1975.

Spivak, Gayatri Chakravorty. *Women's Writing in Exile*. Ed. Mary Lynn Broe and Angela Ingram. Chapel Hill: U of North Carolina P, 1989.

Steedman, Carolyn. *Landscape for a Good Woman*. New Brunswick: Rutgers UP, 1987.

———. *The Tidy House: Little Girls' Writing*. London: Virago, 1982.

Steedman, Carolyn, Cathy Urwin, and Valerie Walkerdine, eds. *Language, Gender and Childhood*. London: Routledge, 1985.

Stephens, John. *Language and Ideology in Children's Fiction*. New York: Longman, 1992.

———. "Metafiction and Interpretation: William Mayne's *Salt River Times, Winter Quarters*, and *Drift*." *Children's Literature* 21 (1993): 101–17.

Stewart, Grace. *A New Mythos: The Novel of the Artist as Heroine 1877–1977*. St. Alban's: Eden, 1979.

Stewig, John W., and Mary L. Knipfel. "Sexism in Picture Books: What Progress?" *Elementary School Journal* 76 (1975): 151–55.

Stout, Janis P. *Strategies of Reticence: Silence and Meaning in the Works of Jane Austen, Willa Cather, Katherine Anne Porter, and Joan Didion*. Charlottesville: UP of Virginia, 1990.

Sutton, Roger. "High School Confidential." *School Library Journal* (December 1985): 43.

Tetenbaum, Toby Jane, and Judith Pearson. "The Voices in Children's Literature: The Impact of Gender on the Moral Decisions of Storybook Characters." *Sex Roles* 20 (1989): 381–95.

Tobin, Patricia. *Time and the Novel: The Genealogical Imperative*. Princeton: Princeton UP, 1978.

Townsend, John Rowe. *Written for Children: An Outline of English Children's Literature*. London: Garnet Miller, 1965.

Trites, Roberta Seelinger. "Claiming the Treasures: Patricia MacLachlan's Organic Postmodernism." *Children's Literature Association Quarterly* 18 (1993): 23–28.

———. "Disney's Sub/Version of Andersen's *Little Mermaid*." *Journal of Popular Film and Television* 18 (1991): 145–52.

———. "Is Flying Extraordinary? Patricia MacLachlan's Use of Aporia." *Children's Literature* 23 (1995): 202–20.

———. "Nesting: Embedded Narratives as Maternal Discourse in Children's Novels." *Children's Literature Association Quarterly* 18 (1993–94): 165–70.

Vallone, Lynn. "'A Humble Spirit under Correction': Tracts, Hymns, and the Ideology of Evangelical Fiction for Children, 1780–1820." *Lion and the Unicorn* 15 (1991): 72–95.

Vandergrift, Kay. "A Feminist Research Agenda in Youth Literature." *Wilson Library Bulletin* (October 1993): 23–27.

Walker, Alice. *In Search of Our Mother's Gardens: Womanist Prose*. New York: Harcourt, 1984.

Waugh, Patricia. *Feminine Fictions: Revisiting the Postmodern*. New York: Routledge, 1989.

————. *Metafictions: The Theory and Practice of Self-Conscious Fiction.* New York: Methuen, 1984.

Weitzman, J., D. Eifler, E. Hokada, and C. Ross. "Sex-Role Socialization in Picture Books for Preschool Children." *American Journal of Sociology* 77 (1972): 1125–50.

Wigutoff, Sharon. "Junior Fiction: A Feminist Critique." *Lion and the Unicorn* 5 (1981): 4–18.

Winnett, Susan. "Coming Unstrung: Women, Men, Narrative, and Principles of Pleasure." *PMLA* 105 (1990): 505–18.

Yarbro-Bejarano, Yvonne. "Chicana Literature from a Chicana Feminist Perspective." *Américas Review* 15 (1987): 139–45.

Zacharias, Lee. "Nancy Drew, Ballbuster." *Journal of Popular Culture* 9 (1975–76): 1027–38.

Zipes, Jack. *Fairy Tales and the Art of Subversion: The Classical Genre for Children and the Process of Civilization.* New York: Wildman, 1983.

INDEX

. . . . . .